May 2015

Dear First-Year Student:

On behalf of President Stuart Rabi.. _ommunity, greetings, and welcome to Hofstra U ....,. iuu are about to join a vibrant, engaged, diverse community, with opportunities ranging from clubs, concerts and athletics to internships and all the cultural events the New York metropolitan area has to offer. First and foremost, however, we are an academic community. At Hofstra, not only will you pursue subjects that already interest you, but our faculty will also spark your interests in new directions.

We use our summer orientation program to give you a taste of the kind of excitement you will experience this fall in a Hofstra classroom. To that end, we are asking all first-year students to read Suzan-Lori Parks's play, *Topdog/Underdog*. We'll discuss it together this summer when you come for orientation. The play won the Pulitzer Prize for drama in 2002 and went on to successful runs on and Off-Broadway and elsewhere. I think as you read it you will see why. It tells the story of two brothers, Lincoln and Booth, whose names were given to them as a joke. It recalls the darkness of the Biblical story of Cain and Abel, with its universal themes of sibling rivalry and resentment—but it transplants these themes into a contemporary context of comedy and race. We know we cannot escape our past, yet we also feel a sense of freedom and responsibility as we confront the future.

To get started, visit hofstra.edu/commonreading. There, you can view video clips of Hofstra faculty and students talking about the book, and you can share your own thoughts about it. If you have questions about the common reading or about New Student Orientation, please call (516)463-4874 or send an e-mail to orientation@hofstra.edu.

I look forward to meeting you this fall.

Sincerely,

Herman A. Berliner, Ph.D.
Provost and Senior Vice President for Academic Affairs

TOPDOG/UNDERDOG

SUZAN-LORI PARKS

THEATRE COMMUNICATIONS GROUP   NEW YORK

Topdog/Underdog is published by Theatre Communications Group, Inc., 520 Eighth Avenue, 24th Floor, New York, NY 10018–4156.

This publication is made possible in part with public funds from the New York State Council on the Arts, a State Agency.

TCG books are exclusively distributed to the book trade by Consortium Book Sales and Distribution.

Library of Congress Cataloging-in-Publication Data

Parks, Suzan-Lori.
Topdog/underdog / Suzan-Lori Parks.— 1st ed.
p. cm.
ISBN-13: 978-1-55936-201-6
ISBN-10: 1-55936-201-4 (pbk. : alk. paper)
1. Brothers—Drama. 2. Sibling rivalry—Drama.
I. Title: Topdog/underdog. II Title.
PS3566.A736 T66   2001
812'.54—dc21   2001027316

Cover design by Pentagram
Text design and composition by Lisa Govan

First Edition, December 2001
Twentieth Printing, January 2023

4 Paul Oscher

who taught me how 2 throw the cards

In January 1999 I was thinking about a play I'd written seven years earlier called *The America Play*. In that play's first act we watch a black man who has fashioned a career for himself: he sits in an arcade impersonating Abraham Lincoln and letting people come and play at shooting him dead—like John Wilkes Booth shot our sixteenth president in 1865 during a performance at Ford's Theatre. So I was thinking about my old play when another black Lincoln impersonator, unrelated to the first guy, came to mind: a new character for a new play. This time I would just focus on his home life. This new Lincoln impersonator's real name would be Lincoln. He would be a former 3-card monte hustler. He would live with his brother, a man named Booth.

My interest in 3-card monte began one day when my husband Paul and I were walking along Canal Street and saw some guys doing the shell game. I was fascinated because, while I'd seen the scam before, this time I had someone whispering a running commentary in my ear, a kind of play-by-play, explaining the ins and outs of the scam, what was really going down. Sure enough the commentator was my husband. Turns out that, back in the days when he played in the Muddy Waters Blues Band, Paul would, for fun, hustle 3-card monte between sets. So when we got home that day he sat me down and showed me how to throw the cards.

This is a play about family wounds and healing. Welcome to the family.

Suzan-Lori Parks
April 2002

Production History

Topdog/Underdog had its world premiere on July 22, 2001, at The Joseph Papp Public Theater/New York Shakespeare Festival (George C. Wolfe, Producer) with support from AT&T:*OnStage*. The director was George C. Wolfe. The scenic design was by Riccardo Hernández, costume design was by Emilio Sosa, lighting design was by Scott Zielinski, sound design was by Dan Moses Schreier, the production stage manager was Rick Steiger and the stage manager was Gwendolyn M. Gilliam. The cast was:

Booth   Don Cheadle
Lincoln   Jeffrey Wright

Topdog/Underdog opened on Broadway at the Ambassador Theatre on April 7, 2002. The director was George C. Wolfe. The scenic design was by Riccardo Hernández, costume design was by Emilio Sosa, lighting design was by Scott Zielinski, sound design was by Dan Moses Schreier, the production stage manager was Rick Steiger and the stage manager was Gwendolyn M. Gilliam. The cast was:

Booth   Mos Def
Lincoln   Jeffrey Wright

TOPDOG/UNDERDOG

The Players

Lincoln
the topdog

Booth
(aka 3-Card), the underdog

Place

here

Time

now

Author's Notes: From the "Elements of Style"

I'm continuing the use of my slightly unconventional theatrical elements. Here's a road map.

- *(Rest)*
  Take a little time, a pause, a breather; make a transition.

- A Spell
  An elongated and heightened *(Rest)*. Denoted by repetition of figures' names with no dialogue. Has sort of an architectural look:

  Lincoln
  Booth
  Lincoln
  Booth

  This is a place where the figures experience their pure true simple state. While no action or stage business is necessary, directors should fill this moment as they best see fit.

- [Brackets in the text indicate optional cuts for production.]

- (Parentheses around dialogue indicate softly spoken passages (asides; sotto voce)).

I am God in nature;

I am a weed by the wall.

—Ralph Waldo Emerson
From "Circles"
Essays: First Series (1841)

Scene One

Thursday evening.
A seedily furnished rooming house room.
A bed, a reclining chair, a small wooden chair,
some other stuff but not much else.
Booth, a black man in his early 30s, practices his
3-card monte scam on the classic setup:
3 playing cards and the cardboard playing board
atop 2 mismatched milk crates.
His moves and accompanying patter are,
for the most part, studied and awkward.

Booth

Watch me close watch me close now: who-see-thuh-red-card-who-see-thuh-red-card? I-see-thuh-red-card. Thuh-red-card-is-thuh-winner. Pick-thuh-red-card-you-pick-uh-winner. Pick-uh-black-card-you-pick-uh-loser. Theres-thuh-loser, yeah, theres-thuh-black-card, theres-thuh-other-loser-and-theres-thuh-red-card, thuh-winner.

(Rest)

Watch me close watch me close now: 3-Card-throws-thuh-cards-lightning-fast. 3-Card-thats-me-and-Ima-last. Watch-me-throw-cause-here-I-go. One-good-pickll-get-you-in, 2-good-picks-and-you-gone-win. See-thuh-red-card-see-thuh-red-card-who-see-thuh-red-card?

(Rest)

Dont touch my cards, man, just point to thuh one you want. You-pick-that-card-you-pick-a-loser, yeah, that-cards-a-loser. You-pick-that-card-thats-thuh-other-loser. You-pick-that-card-you-pick-a-winner. Follow that card. You gotta chase that card. You-pick-thuh-dark-deuce-thats-a-loser-other-dark-deuces-thuh-other-loser, red-deuce, thuh-deuce-of-heartsll-win-it-all. Follow thuh red card.

(Rest)

Ima show you thuh cards: 2 black cards but only one heart. Now watch me now. Who-sees-thuh-red-card-who-knows-where-its-at? Go on, man, point to thuh card. Put yr money down cause you aint no clown. No? Ah you had thuh card, but you didnt have thuh heart.

(Rest)

You wanna bet? 500 dollars? Shoot. You musta been watching 3-Card real close. Ok. Lay the cash in my hand cause 3-Cards thuh man. Thank you, mister. This card you say?

(Rest)

Wrong! Sucker! Fool! Asshole! Bastard! I bet yr daddy heard how stupid you was and drank himself to death just cause he didnt wanna have nothing to do witchu! I bet yr mama seen you when you was born and she wished she was dead, sucker! Ha Ha Ha! And 3-Card, once again, wins all thuh money!!

(Rest)

What? Cops looking my way? Fold up thuh game, and walk away. Sneak outa sight. Set up on another corner.

(Rest)

Yeah.

(Rest)

        Having won the imaginary loot and dodged the
        imaginary cops, Booth sets up his equipment and
        starts practicing his scam all over again.
    Lincoln comes in quietly. He is a black man in his later 30s.
        He is dressed in an antique frock coat and wears
        a top hat and fake beard, that is, he is dressed to look
        like Abraham Lincoln. He surreptitiously walks into
        the room to stand right behind Booth,
        who, engrossed in his cards,
        does not notice Lincoln right away.

Booth

Watch me close watch me close now: who-see-thuh-red-card-who-see-thuh-red-card? I-see-thuh-red-card. Thuh-

red-card-is-thuh-winner. Pick-thuh-red-card-you-pick-uh-winner. Pick-uh-black-card-you-pick-uh-loser. Theres-thuh-loser-yeah-theres-thuh-black-card, theres-thuh-other-loser-and-theres-thuh-red-card, thuh-winner. Don't touch my cards, man, don't—
(Rest)
Dont do that shit. Dont do that shit. Dont do that shit!

> Booth, sensing someone behind him, whirls around,
> pulling a gun from his pants. While the presence of
> Lincoln doesnt surprise him, the Lincoln costume does.

Booth
And woah, man dont *ever* be doing that shit! Who thuh fuck you think you is coming in my shit all spooked out and shit. You pull that one more time I'll shoot you!

Lincoln
I only had a minute to make the bus.

Booth
Bullshit.

Lincoln
Not completely. I mean, its either bull or shit, but not a complete lie so it aint bullshit, right?
(Rest)
Put yr gun away.

Booth
Take off the damn hat at least.

> Lincoln takes off the stovepipe hat.
> Booth puts his gun away.

Lincoln
Its cold out there. This thing kept my head warm.

Booth
I dont like you wearing that bullshit, that shit that bull that disguise that getup that motherdisfuckinguise anywhere in the daddy-dicksticking vicinity of my humble abode.

Lincoln
Better?

Booth
Take off the damn coat too. Damn, man. Bad enough you got to wear that shit all day you come up in here wearing it. What my women gonna say?

Lincoln
What women?

Booth
I got a date with Grace tomorrow. Shes in love with me again but she dont know it yet. Aint no man can love her the way I can. She sees you in that getup its gonna reflect bad on me. She coulda seen you coming down the street. Shit. Could be standing outside right now taking her ring off and throwing it on the sidewalk.

> Booth takes a peek out the window.

Booth
I got her this ring today. Diamond. Well, diamond-esque, but it looks just as good as the real thing. Asked her what size she wore. She say 7 so I go boost a size 6 and a half, right? Show it to her and she loves it and I shove it on her finger and its a tight fit right, so she cant just take it off on a whim, like she did the last one I gave her. Smooth, right?

> Booth takes another peek out the window.

Lincoln
She out there?

Booth
Nope. Coast is clear.

Lincoln
You boosted a ring?

Booth

Yeah. I thought about spending my inheritance on it but—
take off that damn coat, man, you make me nervous standing there looking like a spook, and that damn face paint,
take it off. You should take all of it off at work and leave
it there.

Lincoln

I dont bring it home someone might steal it.

Booth

At least *take it off* there, then.

Lincoln

Yeah.
(Rest)

> Lincoln takes off the frock coat and
> applies cold cream, removing the whiteface.

Lincoln

I was riding the bus. Really I only had a minute to make
my bus and I was sitting in the arcade thinking, should
I change into my street clothes or should I make the bus?
Nobody was in there today anyway. Middle of the week
middle of winter. Not like on weekends. Weekends the place
is packed. So Im riding the bus home. And this kid asked
me for my autograph. I pretended I didnt hear him at first.
I'd had a long day. But he kept asking. Theyd just done
Lincoln in history class and he knew all about him, he'd
been to the arcade but, I dunno, for some reason he was
tripping cause there was Honest Abe right beside him on
the bus. I wanted to tell him to go fuck hisself. But then
I got a look at him. A little rich kid. Born on easy street, you
know the type. So I waited until I could tell he really wanted
it, the autograph, and I told him he could have it for 10
bucks. I was gonna say 5, cause of the Lincoln connection
but something in me made me ask for 10.

Booth

But he didnt have a 10. All he had was a penny. So you took
the penny.

Lincoln
All he had was a *20*. So I took the 20 and told him to meet
me on the bus tomorrow and Honest Abe would give him
the change.

Booth
Shit.

Lincoln
Shit is right.

(Rest)

Booth
Whatd you do with thuh 20?

Lincoln
Bought drinks at Luckys. A round for everybody. They got a
kick out of the getup.

Booth
You shoulda called me down.

Lincoln
Next time, bro.
(Rest)
You making bookshelves? With the milk crates, you making
bookshelves?

Booth
Yeah, big bro, Im making bookshelves.

Lincoln
Whats the cardboard part for?

Booth
Versatility.

Lincoln
Oh.

Booth

I was thinking we dont got no bookshelves we dont got no
dining room table so Im making a sorta modular unit you put
the books in the bottom and the table top on top. We can eat
and store our books. We could put the photo album in there.

Booth gets the raggedy family photo album
and puts it in the milk crate.

Booth

Youd sit there, I'd sit on the edge of the bed. Gathered
around the dinner table. Like old times.

Lincoln

We just gotta get some books but thats great, Booth, thats
real great.

Booth

Dont be calling me Booth no more, K?

Lincoln

You changing yr name?

Booth

Maybe.

Lincoln
Booth

Lincoln

What to?

Booth

Im not ready to reveal it yet.

Lincoln

You already decided on something?

Booth

Maybe.

Lincoln

You gonna call yrself something african? That be cool.
Only pick something thats easy to spell and pronounce,
man, cause you know, some of them african names, I mean,
ok, Im down with the power to the people thing, but, no
ones gonna hire you if they cant say yr name. And some of
them fellas who got they african names, no one can say
they names and they cant say they names neither. I mean,
you dont want yr new handle to obstruct yr employment
possibilities.

Booth
Lincoln

Booth
You bring dinner?

Lincoln
"Shango" would be a good name. The name of the thunder
god. If you aint decided already Im just throwing it in the
pot. I brought chinese.

Booth
Lets try the table out.

Lincoln
Cool.

> They both sit at the new table.
> The food is far away near the door.

Lincoln
Booth

Lincoln
I buy it you set it up. Thats the deal. Thats the deal, right?

Booth
You like this place?

Lincoln
Ssallright.

Booth

But a little cramped sometimes, right?

Lincoln

You dont hear me complain. Although that recliner sometimes Booth, man—no Booth, right—man, Im too old to be
sleeping in that chair.

Booth

Its my place. You dont got a place. Cookie, she threw you
out. And you cant seem to get another woman. Yr lucky
I let you stay.

Lincoln

Every Friday you say *mi casa es su casa.*

Booth

Every Friday you come home with yr paycheck. Today is
Thursday and I tell you brother, its a long way from Friday
to Friday. All kinds of things can happen. All kinds of bad
feelings can surface and erupt while yr little brother waits
for you to bring in yr share.
(Rest)
I got my Thursday head on, Link. Go get the food.

Lincoln doesnt budge.

Lincoln

You dont got no running water in here, man.

Booth

So?

Lincoln

You dont got no toilet you dont got no sink.

Booth

Bathrooms down the hall.

Lincoln

You living in thuh Third World, fool! Hey, I'll get thuh food.

Lincoln goes to get the food.
He sees a stray card on the floor and
examines it without touching it. He brings the food over,
putting it nicely on the table.

Lincoln
You been playing cards?

Booth
Yeah.

Lincoln
Solitaire?

Booth
Thats right. Im getting pretty good at it.

Lincoln
Thats soup and thats sauce. I got you the meat and I got me
the skrimps.

Booth
I wanted the skrimps.

Lincoln
You said you wanted the meat. This morning when I left you
said you wanted the meat.
(Rest)
Here man, take the skrimps. No sweat.

They eat. Chinese food from styrofoam containers,
cans of soda, fortune cookies. Lincoln eats slowly
and carefully, Booth eats ravenously.

Lincoln
Yr getting good at solitaire?

Booth
Yeah. How about we play a hand after eating?

Lincoln
Solitaire?

Booth
Poker or rummy or something.

Lincoln
You know I dont touch thuh cards, man.

Booth
Just for fun.

Lincoln
I dont touch thuh cards.

Booth
How about for money?

Lincoln
You dont got no money. All the money you got I bring in here.

Booth
I got my inheritance.

Lincoln
Thats like saying you dont got no money cause you aint never gonna do nothing with it so its like you dont got it.

Booth
At least I still got mines. You blew yrs.

Lincoln
Booth

Lincoln
You like the skrimps?

Booth
Ssallright.

Lincoln
Whats yr fortune?

Booth
"Waste not want not." Whats yrs?

Lincoln

"Your luck will change!"

> Booth finishes eating. He turns his back to Lincoln
> and fiddles around with the cards, keeping them
> on the bed, just out of Lincolns sight.
> He mutters the 3-card patter under his breath.
> His moves are still clumsy. Every once and a while
> he darts a look over at Lincoln who
> does his best to ignore Booth.

Booth

((((Watch me close watch me close now: who-see-thuh-red-card-who-see-thuh-red-card? I-see-thuh-red-card. Thuh-red-card-is-thuh-winner. Pick-thuh-red-card-you-pick-uh-winner. Pick-uh-black-card-and-you-pick-uh-loser. Theres-thuh-loser, yeah, theres-thuh-black-card, theres-thuh-other-loser-and-theres-thuh-red-card, thuh-winner! Cop C, Stick, Cop C! Go on—))))

Lincoln

((Shit.))

Booth

(((((((One-good-pickll-get-you-in, 2-good-picks-and-you-gone-win. Dont touch my cards, man, just point to thuh one you want. You-pick-that-card-you-pick-uh-loser, yeah, that-cards-uh-loser. You-pick-that-card-thats-thuh-other-loser. You-pick-that-card-you-pick-uh-winner. Follow-that-card. You-gotta-chase-that-card!)))))))

Lincoln

You wanna hustle 3-card monte, you gotta do it right, you gotta break it down. Practice it in smaller bits. Yr trying to do the whole thing at once thats why you keep fucking it up.

Booth

Show me.

Lincoln

No. Im just saying you wanna do it you gotta do it right and if you gonna do it right you gotta work on it in smaller bits, thatsall.

Booth

You and me could team up and do it together. We'd clean up, Link.

Lincoln

I'll clean up—bro.

Lincoln cleans up. As he clears the food, Booth goes back to using the "table" for its original purpose.

Booth

My new names 3-Card. 3-Card, got it? You wanted to know it so now you know it. 3-card monte by 3-Card. Call me 3-Card from here on out.

Lincoln

3-Card. Shit.

Booth

Im getting everybody to call me 3-Card. Grace likes 3-Card better than Booth. She says 3-Cards got something to it. Anybody not calling me 3-Card gets a bullet.

Lincoln

Yr too much, man.

Booth

Im making a point.

Lincoln

Point made, 3-Card. Point made.

Lincoln picks up his guitar. Plays at it.

Booth

Oh, come on, man, we could make money you and me. Throwing down the cards. 3-Card and Link: look out! We could clean up you and me. You would throw the cards and I'd be yr Stickman. The one in the crowd who looks like just an innocent passerby, who looks like just another player, like just another customer, but who gots intimate connec-

tions with you, the Dealer, the one throwing the cards, the
main man. I'd be the one who brings in the crowd, I'd be the
one who makes them want to put they money down, you
do yr moves and I do mines. You turn yr head and I turn
the card—

Lincoln
It aint as easy as all that. Theres—

Booth
We could be a team, man. Rake in the money! Sure thered
be some cats out there with fast eyes, some brothers and
sisters who would watch real close and pick the right card,
and so thered be some days when we would lose money,
but most of the days we would come out on top! Pockets
bulging, plenty of cash! And the ladies would be thrilling!
You could afford to get laid! Grace would be all over me again.

Lincoln
I thought you said she was all over you.

Booth
She is she is. Im seeing her tomorrow but today we gotta
solidify the shit twixt you and me. Big brother Link and
little brother Booth—

Lincoln
3-Card.

Booth
Yeah. Scheming and dreaming. No one throws the cards like
you, Link. And with yr moves and my magic, and we get
Grace and a girl for you to round out the posse. We'd be
golden, bro! Am I right?

Lincoln
Lincoln

Booth
Am I right?

Lincoln

I dont touch thuh cards, 3-Card. I dont touch thuh cards no more.

Lincoln
Booth
Lincoln
Booth

Booth

You know what Mom told me when she was packing to leave? You was at school motherfucker you was at school. You got up that morning and sat down in yr regular place and read the cereal box while Dad read the sports section and Mom brought you yr dick toast and then you got on the damn school bus cause you didnt have the sense to do nothing else you was so into yr own shit that you didnt have the sense to feel nothing else going on. I had the sense to go back cause I was feeling something going on man, I was feeling something changing. So I—

Lincoln

Cut school that day like you did almost every day—

Booth

She was putting her stuff in bags. She had all them nice suitcases but she was putting her stuff in bags.
(Rest)
Packing up her shit. She told me to look out for you. I told her I was the little brother and the big brother should look out after the little brother. She just said it again. That I should look out for you. Yeah. So who gonna look out for me. Not like you care. Here I am interested in an economic opportunity, willing to work hard, willing to take risks and all you can say you shiteating motherfucking pathetic limpdick uncle tom, all you can tell me is how you dont do no more what I be wanting to do. Here I am trying to earn a living and you standing in my way. YOU STANDING IN MY WAY, LINK!

Lincoln

Im sorry.

Booth
Yeah, you sorry all right.

Lincoln
I cant be hustling no more, bro.

Booth
What you do all day aint no hustle?

Lincoln
Its honest work.

Booth
Dressing up like some crackerass white man, some dead president and letting people shoot at you sounds like a hustle to me.

Lincoln
People know the real deal. When people know the real deal it aint a hustle.

Booth
We do the card game people will know the real deal. Sometimes we will win sometimes they will win. They fast they win, we faster we win.

Lincoln
I aint going back to that, bro. I aint going back.

Booth
You play Honest Abe. You aint going back but you going all the way back. Back to way back then when folks was slaves and shit.

Lincoln
Dont push me.

Booth
Lincoln

Booth
You gonna have to leave.

Lincoln
I'll be gone tomorrow.

Booth
Good. Cause this was only supposed to be a temporary arrangement.

Lincoln
I will be gone tomorrow.

Booth
Good.

> Booth sits on his bed. Lincoln, sitting in his easy chair
> with his guitar, plays and sings.

Lincoln
My dear mother left me, my fathers gone away
My dear mother left me and my fathers gone away
I dont got no money, I dont got no place to stay.

My best girl, she threw me out into the street
My favorite horse, they ground him into meat
Im feeling cold from my head down to my feet.

My luck was bad but now it turned to worse
My luck was bad but now it turned to worse
Dont call me up a doctor, just call me up a hearse.

Booth
You just made that up?

Lincoln
I had it in my head for a few days.

Booth
Sounds good.

Lincoln
Thanks.
(Rest)
Daddy told me once why we got the names we do.

Booth
Yeah?

Lincoln
Yeah.
(Rest)
He was drunk when he told me, or maybe I was drunk when he told me. Anyway he told me, may not be true, but he told me. Why he named us both. Lincoln and Booth.

Booth
How come. How come, man?

Lincoln
It was his idea of a joke.

Both men relax back as the lights fade.

Scene Two

Friday evening.
The very next day.
Booth comes in looking like he is
bundled up against the cold.
He makes sure his brother isnt home, then stands
in the middle of the room. From his big coat sleeves
he pulls out one new shoe then another,
from another sleeve come two more shoes.
He then slithers out a belt from each sleeve.
He removes his coat. Underneath he wears a very nice
new suit. He removes the jacket and pants
revealing another new suit underneath. The suits still have
the price tags on them. He takes two neckties
from his pockets and two folded shirts
from the back of his pants. He pulls a magazine
from the front of his pants. Hes clearly
had a busy day of shoplifting.
He lays one suit out on Lincolns easy chair.
The other he lays out on his own bed.
He goes out into the hall returning with a folding screen
which he sets up between the bed and
the recliner creating 2 separate spaces.
He takes out a bottle of whiskey and two glasses,
setting them on the two stacked milk crates.
He hears footsteps and sits down in the
small wooden chair reading the magazine.
Lincoln, dressed in street clothes, comes in.

Lincoln
Taaaaadaaaaaaaa!

Booth

Lordamighty, Pa, I smells money!

Lincoln

Sho nuff, Ma. Poppas brung home thuh bacon.

Booth

Bringitherebringitherebringithere.

> With a series of very elaborate moves
> Lincoln brings the money over to Booth.

Booth

Put it in my hands, Pa!

Lincoln

I want ya tuh smells it first, Ma!

Booth

Put it neath my nose then, Pa!

Lincoln

Take yrself a good long whiff of them greenbacks.

Booth

Oh lordamighty Ima faint, Pa! Get me muh med-sin!

> Lincoln quickly pours two large glasses of whiskey.

Lincoln

Dont die on me, Ma!

Booth

Im fading fast, Pa!

Lincoln

Thinka thuh children, Ma! Thinka thuh farm!

Booth

1-2-3.

Both men gulp down their drinks simultaneously.

Lincoln and Booth
AAAAAAAAAAAAAAAAAAAAAH!

Lots of laughing and slapping on the backs.

Lincoln
Budget it out man budget it out.

Booth
You in a hurry?

Lincoln
Yeah. I wanna see how much we got for the week.

Booth
You rush in here and dont even look around. Could be a fucking A-bomb in the middle of the floor you wouldnt notice. Yr wife, Cookie—

Lincoln
X-wife—

Booth
—could be in my bed you wouldnt notice—

Lincoln
She was once—

Booth
Look the fuck around please.

Lincoln looks around and sees the new suit on his chair.

Lincoln
Wow.

Booth
Its yrs.

Lincoln
Shit.

Booth
Got myself one too.

Lincoln
Boosted?

Booth
Yeah, I boosted em. Theys stole from a big-ass department store. That store takes in more money in one day than we will in our whole life. I stole and I stole generously. I got one for me and I got one for you. Shoes belts shirts ties socks in the shoes and everything. Got that screen too.

Lincoln
You all right, man.

Booth
Just cause I aint good as you at cards dont mean I cant do nothing.

Lincoln
Lets try em on.

> They stand in their separate sleeping spaces,
> Booth near his bed, Lincoln near his recliner,
> and try on their new clothes.

Booth
Ima wear mine tonight. Gracell see me in this and *she* gonna ask me tuh marry *her*.
(Rest)
I got you the blue and I got me the brown. I walked in there and walked out and they didnt as much as bat an eye. Thats how smooth lil bro be, Link.

Lincoln
You did good. You did real good, 3-Card.

Booth

All in a days work.

Lincoln

They say the clothes make the man. All day long I wear that getup. But that dont make me who I am. Old black coat not even real old just fake old. Its got worn spots on the elbows, little raggedy places thatll break through into holes before the winters out. Shiny strips around the cuffs and the collar. Dust from the cap guns on the left shoulder where they shoot him, where they shoot me I should say but I never feel like they shooting me. The fella who had the gig before I had it wore the same coat. When I got the job they had the getup hanging there waiting for me. Said thuh fella before me just took it off one day and never came back.
(Rest)
Remember how Dads clothes used to hang in the closet?

Booth

Until you took em outside and burned em.
(Rest)
He had some nice stuff. What he didnt spend on booze he spent on women. What he didnt spend on them two he spent on clothes. He had some nice stuff. I would look at his stuff and calculate thuh how long it would take till I was big enough to fit it. Then you went and burned it all up.

Lincoln

I got tired of looking at em without him in em.
(Rest)
They said thuh fella before me—he took off the getup one day, hung it up real nice, and never came back. And as they offered me thuh job, saying of course I would have to wear a little makeup and accept less than what they would offer a—another guy—

Booth

Go on, say it. "White." Theyd pay you less than theyd pay a white guy.

Lincoln

I said to myself thats exactly what I would do: wear it out and then leave it hanging there and not come back. But until then, I would make a living at it. But it dont make me. Worn suit coat, not even worn by the fool that Im supposed to be playing, but making fools out of all those folks who come crowding in for they chance to play at something great. Fake beard. Top hat. Dont make me into no Lincoln. I was Lincoln on my own before any of that.

The men finish dressing. They style and profile.

Booth

Sharp, huh?

Lincoln

Very sharp.

Booth

You look sharp too, man. You look like the real you. Most of the time you walking around all bedraggled and shit. You look good. Like you used to look back in thuh day when you had Cookie in love with you and all the women in the world was eating out of yr hand.

Lincoln

This is real nice, man. I dont know where Im gonna wear it but its real nice.

Booth

Just wear it around. Itll make you feel good and when you feel good yll meet someone nice. Me I aint interested in meeting no one nice, I mean, I only got eyes for Grace. You think she'll go for me in this?

Lincoln

I think thuh tie you gave me'll go better with what you got on.

Booth

Yeah?

Lincoln

Grace likes bright colors dont she? My ties bright, yrs is too subdued.

Booth

Yeah. Gimmie yr tie.

Lincoln

You gonna take back a gift?

Booth

I stole the damn thing didnt I? Gimmie yrs! I'll give you mines.

> They switch neckties. Booth is pleased.
> Lincoln is *more* pleased.

Lincoln

Do thuh budget.

Booth

Right. Ok lets see: we got 314 dollars. We put 100 aside for the rent. 100 a week times 4 weeks makes the rent and—

Lincoln and Booth

—we dont want thuh rent spent.

Booth

That leaves 214. We put aside 30 for the electric leaving 184. We put aside 50 for thuh phone leaving 134.

Lincoln

We dont got a phone.

Booth

We pay our bill theyll turn it back on.

Lincoln

We dont need no phone.

Booth

How you gonna get a woman if you dont got a phone? Women these days are more cautious, more whaddacallit, more circumspect. You go into a club looking like a fast daddy, you get a filly to give you her numerophono and gone is the days when she just gives you her number and dont ask for yrs.

Lincoln
Like a woman is gonna call me.

Booth
She dont wanna call you she just doing a preliminary survey of the property. Shit, Link, you dont know nothin no more.
(Rest)
She gives you her number and she asks for yrs. You give her yr number. The phone number of yr home. Thereby telling her 3 things: 1) you got a home, that is, you aint no smooth talking smooth dressing *homeless* joe; 2) that you is in possession of a telephone and a working telephone number which is to say that you got thuh cash and thuh wherewithal to acquire for yr self the worlds most revolutionary communication apparatus and you together enough to pay yr bills!

Lincoln
Whats 3?

Booth
You give her yr number you telling her that its cool to call if she should so please, that is, that you aint got no wife or wife approximation on the premises.
(Rest)
50 for the phone leaving 134. We put aside 40 for "med-sin."

Lincoln
The price went up. 2 bucks more a bottle.

Booth
We'll put aside 50, then. That covers the bills. We got 84 left. 40 for meals together during the week leaving 44. 30 for me 14 for you. I got a woman I gotta impress tonight.

Lincoln
You didnt take out for the phone last week.

Booth

Last week I was depressed. This week things is looking up. For both of us.

Lincoln

Theyre talking about cutbacks at the arcade. I only been there 8 months, so—

Booth

Dont sweat it man, we'll find something else.

Lincoln

Not nothing like this. I like the job. This is sit down, you know, easy work. I just gotta sit there all day. Folks come in kill phony Honest Abe with the phony pistol. I can sit there and let my mind travel.

Booth

Think of women.

Lincoln

Sometimes.
(Rest)
All around the whole arcade is buzzing and popping. Thuh whirring of thuh duckshoot, baseballs smacking the back wall when someone misses the stack of cans, some woman getting happy cause her fella just won the ring toss. The Boss playing the barker talking up the fake freaks. The smell of the ocean and cotton candy and rat shit. And in thuh middle of all that, I can just sit and let my head go quiet. Make up songs, make plans. Forget.
(Rest)
You should come down again.

Booth

Once was plenty, but thanks.
(Rest)
Yr Best Customer, he come in today?

Lincoln

Oh, yeah, he was there.

Booth
He shoot you?

Lincoln
He shot Honest Abe, yeah.

Booth
He talk to you?

Lincoln
In a whisper. Shoots on the left whispers on the right.

Booth
Whatd he say this time?

Lincoln
"Does thuh show stop when no ones watching or does thuh show go on?"

Booth
Hes getting deep.

Lincoln
Yeah.

Booth
Whatd he say, that one time? "Yr only yrself—"

Lincoln
"—when no ones watching," yeah.

Booth
Thats deep shit.
(Rest)
Hes a brother, right?

Lincoln
I think so.

Booth
He know yr a brother?

Lincoln

I dunno.

Booth

Hes a *deep* black brother.

Lincoln

Yeah. He makes the day interesting.

Booth

(Rest)

Thats a fucked-up job you got.

Lincoln

Its a living.

Booth

But you aint living.

Lincoln

Im alive aint I?

(Rest)

One day I was throwing the cards. Next day Lonny died. Somebody shot him. I knew I was next, so I quit. I saved my life.

(Rest)

The arcade gig is the first lucky break Ive ever had. And Ive actually grown to like the work. And now theyre talking about cutting me.

Booth

You was lucky with thuh cards.

Lincoln

Lucky? Aint nothing lucky about cards. Cards aint luck. Cards is work. Cards is skill. Aint never nothing lucky about cards.

(Rest)

I dont wanna lose my job.

Booth

Then you gotta jazz up yr act. Elaborate yr moves, you
know. You was always too stiff with it. You cant just sit
there! Maybe, when they shoot you, you know, leap up flail
yr arms then fall down and wiggle around and shit so they
gotta shoot you more than once. Blam Blam Blam! Blam!

Lincoln

Help me practice. I'll sit here like I do at work and you be
like one of the tourists.

Booth

No thanks.

Lincoln

My paychecks on the line, man.

Booth

I got a date. Practice on yr own.
(Rest)
I got a rendezvous with Grace. Shit she so sweet she makes
my teeth hurt.
(Rest)
Link, uh, howbout slipping me an extra 5 spot. Its the
biggest night of my life.

Lincoln
Booth

Lincoln gives Booth a 5er.

Booth

Thanks.

Lincoln

No sweat.

Booth

Howabout I run through it with you when I get back. Put on
yr getup and practice till then.

Lincoln
Sure.

> Booth leaves. Lincoln stands there alone.
> He takes off his shoes, giving them a shine.
> He takes off his socks and his fancy suit,
> hanging it neatly over the little wooden chair.
> He takes his getup out of his shopping bag. He puts it on,
> slowly, like an actor preparing for a great role:
> frock coat, pants, beard, top hat, necktie.
> He leaves his feet bare. The top hat has an elastic band
> which he positions securely underneath his chin.
> He picks up the white pancake makeup
> but decides against it.
> He sits. He pretends to get shot,
> flings himself on the floor and thrashes around.
> He gets up, considers giving the new moves another try,
> but instead pours himself a big glass of whiskey
> and sits there drinking.

Scene Three

Much later that same Friday evening. The recliner
is reclined to its maximum horizontal position
and Lincoln lies there asleep.
He wakes with a start. He is horrific,
bleary eyed and hungover, in his full Lincoln regalia.
He takes a deep breath, realizes where he is
and reclines again, going back to sleep.
Booth comes in full of swagger. He slams the door
trying to wake his brother who is dead to the world.
He opens the door and slams it again. This time Lincoln
wakes up, as hungover and horrid as before.
Booth swaggers about, his moves are exaggerated,
rooster-like. He walks round and round Lincoln
making sure his brother sees him.

Lincoln
You hurt yrself?

Booth
I had me "an evening to remember."

Lincoln
You look like you hurt yrself.

Booth
Grace Grace Grace. *Grace*. She wants me back. She wants
me back so bad she wiped her hand over the past where we
wasnt together just so she could say we aint never been
apart. She wiped her hand over our breakup. She wiped
her hand over her childhood, her teenage years, her first

boyfriend, just so she could say that she been mine since the dawn of time.

Lincoln
Thats great, man.

Booth
And all the shit I put her through: she wiped it clean. And the women I saw while I was seeing her—

Lincoln
Wiped clean too?

Booth
Mister Clean, Mister, Mister Clean!

Lincoln
Whered you take her?

Booth
We was over at her place. I brought thuh food. Stopped at the best place I could find and stuffed my coat with only the best. We had the music we had the candlelight we had—

Lincoln
She let you do it?

Booth
Course she let me do it.

Lincoln
She let you do it without a rubber?

Booth
—Yeah.

Lincoln
Bullshit.

Booth
I put my foot down—and she *melted*. And she was—huh— she was something else. I dont wanna get you jealous, though.

Lincoln

Go head, I dont mind.

Booth

(Rest)
Well, you know what she looks like.

Lincoln

She walks on by and the emergency room fills up cause all the guys get whiplash from lookin at her.

Booth

Thats right thats right. Well—she comes to the door wearing nothing but her little nightie, eats up the food I'd brought like there was no tomorrow and then goes and eats on me.
(Rest)

Lincoln

Go on.

Booth

I dont wanna make you feel bad, man.

Lincoln

Ssallright. Go on.

Booth

(Rest)
Well, uh, you know what shes like. Wild. Goodlooking. So sweet my teeth hurt.

Lincoln

A sexmachine.

Booth

Yeah.

Lincoln

A hotsy-totsy.

Booth

Yeah.

Lincoln
Amazing Grace.

Booth
Amazing Grace! Yeah. Thats right. She let me do her how
I wanted. And no rubber.
(Rest)

Lincoln
Go on.

Booth
You dont wanna hear the mushy shit.

Lincoln
Sure I do.

Booth
You hate mushy shit. You always hated thuh mushy shit.

Lincoln
Ive changed. Go head. You had "an evening to remember,"
remember? I was just here alone sitting here. Drinking.
Go head. Tell Link thuh stink.
(Rest)
Howd ya do her?

Booth
Dogstyle.

Lincoln
Amazing Grace.

Booth
In front of a mirror.

Lincoln
So you could see her. Her face her breasts her back her ass.
Graces got a great ass.

Booth
Its all right.

Lincoln
Amazing Grace!

> Booth goes into his bed area and takes off his suit,
> tossing the clothes on the floor.

Booth
She said next time Ima have to use a rubber. She let me
have my way this time but she said that next time I'd have
to put my boots on.

Lincoln
Im sure you can talk her out of it.

Booth
Yeah.
(Rest)
What kind of rubbers you use, I mean, when you was with
Cookie.

Lincoln
We didnt use rubbers. We was married, man.

Booth
Right. But you had other women on the side. What kind you
use when you was with them?

Lincoln
Magnums.

Booth
Thats thuh kind I picked up. For next time. Grace was real
strict about it. Magnums.

> While Booth sits on his bed fiddling with his
> box of condoms, Lincoln sits in his chair
> and resumes drinking.

Lincoln
Theyre for "the larger man."

Booth
Right. Right.

> Lincoln keeps drinking as Booth, sitting in the privacy
> of his bedroom, fiddles with the condoms,
> perhaps trying to put one on.

Lincoln
Thats right.

Booth
Graces real different from them fly-by-night gals I was
making do with. Shes in school. Making something of
herself. Studying cosmetology. You should see what she
can do with a womans hair and nails.

Lincoln
Too bad you aint a woman.

Booth
What?

Lincoln
You could get yrs done for free, I mean.

Booth
Yeah. She got this way of sitting. Of talking. That. Every-
thing she does is. Shes just so hot.
(Rest)
We was together 2 years. Then we broke up. I had my little
employment difficulty and she needed time to think.

Lincoln
And shes through thinking now.

Booth
Thats right.

Lincoln
Booth

Lincoln
Whatcha doing back there?

Booth
Resting. That girl wore me out.

Lincoln
You want some med-sin?

Booth
No thanks.

Lincoln
Come practice my moves with me, then.

Booth
Lets hit it tomorrow, K?

Lincoln
I been waiting. I got all dressed up and you said if I waited
up—come on, man, they gonna replace me with a wax dummy.

Booth
No shit.

Lincoln
Thats what theyre talking about. Probably just talk, but—
come on, man, I even lent you 5 bucks.

Booth
Im tired.

Lincoln
You didnt get shit tonight.

Booth
You jealous, man. You just jail-us.

Lincoln
You laying over there yr balls blue as my boosted suit.
Laying over there waiting for me to go back to sleep or black
out so I wont hear you rustling thuh pages of yr fuck book.

Booth

Fuck you, man.

Lincoln

I was over there looking for something the other week and theres like 100 fuck books under yr bed and theyre matted together like a bad fro, bro, cause you spunked in the pages and didnt wipe them off.

Booth

Im hot. I need constant sexual release. If I wasnt taking care of myself by myself I would be out there running around on thuh town which costs cash that I dont have so I would be doing worse: I'd be out there doing who knows what, shooting people and shit. Out of a need for unresolved sexual release. I'm a hot man. I aint apologizing for it. When I dont got a woman, I gotta make do. Not like you, Link. When you dont got a woman you just sit there. Letting yr shit fester. Yr dick, if it aint falled off yet, is hanging there between yr legs, little whiteface shriveled-up blank-shooting grub worm. As goes thuh man so goes thuh mans dick. Thats what I say. Least my shits intact.
(Rest)
You a limp dick jealous whiteface motherfucker whose wife dumped him cause he couldnt get it up and she told me so. Came crawling to me cause she needed a man.
(Rest)
I gave it to Grace good tonight. So goodnight.

Lincoln
(Rest)
Goodnight.

Lincoln
Booth
Lincoln
Booth
Lincoln
Booth

Lincoln sitting in his chair. Booth lying in bed.
Time passes.
Booth peeks out to see if Lincoln is asleep.
Lincoln is watching for him.

Lincoln
You can hustle 3-card monte without me you know.

Booth
Im planning to.

Lincoln
I could contact my old crew. You could work with them.
Lonny aint around no more but theres the rest of them.
Theyre good.

Booth
I can get my own crew. I dont need yr crew. Buncha has-
beens. I can get my own crew.

Lincoln
My crews experienced. We usedta pull down a thousand a
day. Thats 7 G a week. That was years ago. They probably
do twice, 3 times that now.

Booth
I got my own connections, thank you.

Lincoln
Theyd take you on in a heartbeat. With my say. My say still
counts with them. They know you from before, when you
tried to hang with us but—wernt ready yet. They know you
from then, but I'd talk you up. I'd say yr my bro, which they
know, and I'd say youd been working the west coast. Little
towns. Mexican border. Taking tourists. I'd tell them you got
moves like I dreamed of having. Meanwhile youd be working
out yr shit right here, right in this room, getting good and
getting better every day so when I did do the reintroductions
youd have some marketable skills. Youd be passable.

Booth
I'd be more than passable, I'd be the be all end all.

Lincoln

Youd be the be all end all. And youd have my say. If yr interested.

Booth

Could do.

Lincoln

Youd have to get a piece. They all pack pistols, bro.

Booth

I *got* a piece.

Lincoln

Youd have to be packing something more substantial than that pop gun, 3-Card. These hustlers is upper echelon hustlers they pack upper echelon heat, not no Saturday night shit, now.

Booth

Whata you know of heat? You aint hung with those guys for 6, 7 years. You swore off em. Threw yr heat in thuh river and you "Dont touch thuh cards." I know more about heat than you know about heat.

Lincoln

Im around guns every day. At the arcade. Theyve all been reworked so they only fire caps but I see guns every day. Lots of guns.

Booth

What kinds?

Lincoln

You been there, you seen them. Shiny deadly metal each with their own deadly personality.

Booth

Maybe I *could* visit you over there. I'd boost one of them guns and rework it to make it shoot for real again. What kind you think would best suit my personality?

Lincoln

You aint stealing nothing from the arcade.

Booth

I go in there and steal if I want to go in there and steal I go in there and steal.

Lincoln

It aint worth it. They dont shoot nothing but blanks.

Booth

Yeah, like you. Shooting blanks.
(Rest)
(Rest)
You ever wonder if someones gonna come in there with a real gun? A real gun with real slugs? Someone with uh axe tuh grind or something?

Lincoln

No.

Booth

Someone who hates you come in there and guns you down and gets gone before anybody finds out.

Lincoln

I dont got no enemies.

Booth

Yr X.

Lincoln

Cookie dont hate me.

Booth

Yr Best Customer? Some miscellaneous stranger?

Lincoln

I cant be worrying about the actions of miscellaneous strangers.

Booth

But there they come day in day out for a chance to shoot
Honest Abe.
(Rest)
Who are they mostly?

Lincoln

I dont really look.

Booth

You must see something.

Lincoln

Im supposed to be staring straight ahead. Watching a play,
like Abe was.

Booth

All day goes by and you never ever take a sneak peek at
who be pulling the trigger.

> Pulled in by his own curiosity, Booth has come out
> of his bed area to stand on the dividing line
> between the two spaces.

Lincoln

Its pretty dark. To keep thuh illusion of thuh whole thing.
(Rest)
But on thuh wall opposite where I sit theres a little electrical
box, like a fuse box. Silver metal. Its got uh dent in it like
somebody hit it with they fist. Big old dent so everything
reflected in it gets reflected upside down. Like yr looking
in uh spoon. And thats where I can see em. The assassins.
(Rest)
Not behind me yet but I can hear him coming. Coming in
with his gun in hand, thuh gun he already picked out up
front when he paid his fare. Coming on in. But not behind
me yet. His dress shoes making too much noise on the
carpet, the carpets too thin, Boss should get a new one but
hes cheap. Not behind me yet. Not behind me yet. Cheap
lightbulb just above my head.
(Rest)

And there he is. Standing behind me. Standing in position.
Standing upside down. Theres some feet shapes on the floor
so he knows just where he oughta stand. So he wont miss.
Thuh gun is always cold. Winter or summer thuh gun is
always cold. And when the gun touches me he can feel that
Im warm and he knows Im alive. And if Im alive then he
can shoot me dead. And for a minute, with him hanging back
there behind me, its real. Me looking at him upside down
and him looking at me looking like Lincoln. Then he shoots.
(Rest)
I slump down and close my eyes. And he goes out thuh
other way. More come in. Uh whole day full. Bunches of
kids, little good for nothings, in they school uniforms.
Businessmen smelling like two for one martinis. Tourists
in they theme park t-shirts trying to catch it on film.
Housewives with they mouths closed tight, shooting
more than once.
(Rest)
They all get so into it. I do my best for them. And now they
talking bout cutting me, replacing me with uh wax dummy.

Booth
You just gotta show yr boss that you can do things a wax
dummy cant do. You too dry with it. You gotta add spicy shit.

Lincoln
Like what.

Booth
Like when they shoot you, I dunno, scream or something.

Lincoln
Scream?

> Booth plays the killer without using his gun.

Booth
Try it. I'll be the killer. Bang!

Lincoln
Aaaah!

Booth
Thats good.

Lincoln
A wax dummy can scream. They can put a voicebox in it and make it like its screaming.

Booth
You can curse. Try it. Bang!

Lincoln
Motherfucking cocksucker!

Booth
Thats good, man.

Lincoln
They aint going for that, though.

Booth
You practice rolling and wiggling on the floor?

Lincoln
A little.

Booth
Lemmie see. Bang!

> Lincoln slumps down, falls on the floor
> and silently wiggles around.

Booth
You look more like a worm on the sidewalk. Move yr arms. Good. Now scream or something.

Lincoln
Aaaah! Aaaaah! Aaaah!

Booth
A little tougher than that, you sound like yr fucking.

Lincoln

Aaaaaah!

Booth

Hold yr head or something, where I shotcha. Good. And look at me! I am the assassin! *I am Booth!!* Come on man this is life and death! Go all out!

Lincoln goes all out.

Booth

Cool, man thats cool. Thats enough.

Lincoln

Whatdoyathink?

Booth

I dunno, man. Something about it. I dunno. It was looking too real or something.

Lincoln

Goddamn you! They dont want it looking too real. I'd scare the customers. Then I'd be out for sure. Yr trying to get me fired.

Booth

Im trying to help. Cross my heart.

Lincoln

People are funny about they Lincoln shit. Its historical. People like they historical shit in a certain way. They like it to unfold the way they folded it up. Neatly like a book. Not raggedy and bloody and screaming. You trying to get me fired.
(Rest)
I am uh brother playing Lincoln. Its uh stretch for anyones imagination. And it aint easy for me neither. Every day I put on that shit, I leave my own shit at the door and I put on that shit and I go out there and I make it work. I make it look easy but its hard. That shit is hard. But it works. Cause I work it. And you trying to get me fired.
(Rest)

I swore off them cards. Took nowhere jobs. Drank. Then
Cookie threw me out. What thuh fuck was I gonna do?
I seen that "Help Wanted" sign and I went up in there and
I looked good in the getup and agreed to the whiteface and
they really dug it that me and Honest Abe got the same name.
(Rest)
Its a sit down job. With benefits. I dont wanna get fired.
They wont give me a good reference if I get fired.

Booth
Iffen you was tuh get fired, then, well—then you and me
could—hustle the cards together. We'd have to support our-
selves somehow.
(Rest)
Just show me how to do the hook part of the card hustle,
man. The part where the Dealer looks away but somehow he
sees—

Lincoln
I couldnt remember if I wanted to.

Booth
Sure you could.

Lincoln
No.
(Rest)
Night, man.

Booth
Yeah.

> Lincoln stretches out in his recliner.
> Booth stands over him waiting for him to get up,
> to change his mind. But Lincoln is fast asleep.
> Booth covers him with a blanket then goes to his bed,
> turning off the lights as he goes. He quietly rummages
> underneath his bed for a girlie magazine which,
> as the lights fade, he reads with great interest.

Scene Four

Saturday.
Just before dawn.
Lincoln gets up. Looks around.
Booth is fast asleep, dead to the world.

Lincoln

No fucking running water.

He stumbles around the room looking for something
which he finally finds: a plastic cup, which he uses as a urinal.
He finishes peeing and finds an out of the way place
to stow the cup. He claws at his Lincoln getup,
removing it and tearing it in the process.
He strips down to his t-shirt and shorts.

Lincoln

Hate falling asleep in this damn shit. Shit. Ripped the beard.
I can just hear em tomorrow. Busiest day of the week. They
looking me over to make sure Im presentable. They got a slew
of guys working but Im the only one they look over every day.
"Yr beards ripped, pal. Sure, we'll getcha new one but its
gonna be coming outa yr pay." Shit. I should quit right then
and there. I'd yank off the beard, throw it on the ground and
stomp it, then go strangle the fucking boss. Thatd be good.
My hands around his neck and his bug eyes bugging out.
You been ripping me off since I took this job and now Im
gonna have to take it outa *yr* pay, motherfucker. Shit.
(Rest)
Sit down job. With benefits.
(Rest)

Hustling. Shit, I was good. I was great. Hell I was the be all end all. I was throwing cards like throwing cards was made for me. Made for me and me alone. I was the best anyone ever seen. Coast to coast. Everybody said so. And I never lost. Not once. Not one time. Not never. Thats how much them cards was mines. I was the be all end all. I was that good.

(Rest)

Then you woke up one day and you didnt have the taste for it no more. Like something in you knew—. Like something in you knew it was time to quit. Quit while you was still ahead. Something in you was telling you—. But hells no. Not Link thuh stink. So I went out there and threw one more time. What thuh fuck. And Lonny died.

(Rest)

Got yrself a good job. And when the arcade lets you go yll get another good job. I dont gotta spend my whole life hustling. Theres more to Link than that. More to me than some cheap hustle. More to life than cheating some idiot out of his paycheck or his life savings.

(Rest)

Like that joker and his wife from out of town. Always wanted to see the big city. I said you could see the bigger end of the big city with a little more cash. And if they was fast enough, faster than me, and here I slowed down my moves I slowed em way down and my Lonny, my right hand, my Stickman, Lonny could draw a customer in like nothing else, Lonny could draw a fly from fresh shit, he could draw Adam outa Eve just with that look he had, Lonny always got folks playing.

(Rest)

Somebody shot him. They dont know who. Nobody knows nobody cares.

(Rest)

We took that man and his wife for hundreds. No, thousands. We took them for everything they had and everything they ever wanted to have. We took a father for the money he was gonna get his kids new bike with and he cried in the street while we vanished. We took a mothers welfare check, she pulled a knife on us and we ran. She threw it but her aim werent shit. People shopping. Greedy. Thinking they could take me and they got took instead.

(Rest)
Swore off thuh cards. Something inside me telling me—.
But I was good.

Lincoln
Lincoln

> He sees a packet of cards.
> He studies them like an alcoholic would study a drink.
> Then he reaches for them, delicately picking them up
> and choosing 3 cards.

Lincoln
Still got my moves. Still got my touch. Still got my chops.
Thuh feel of it. And I aint hurting no one, God. Link is just
here hustling hisself.
(Rest)
Lets see whatcha got.

> He stands over the monte setup. Then he bends over it
> placing the cards down and moving them around.
> Slowly at first, aimlessly,
> as if hes just making little ripples in water.
> But then the game draws him in.
> Unlike Booth, Lincolns patter and moves are
> deft, dangerous, electric.

Lincoln
(((Lean in close and watch me now: who see thuh black card
who see thuh black card I see thuh black card black cards
thuh winner pick thuh black card thats thuh winner pick
thuh red card thats thuh loser pick thuh other red card thats
thuh other loser pick thuh black card you pick thuh winner.
Watch me as I throw thuh cards. Here we go.)))
(Rest)
(((Who see thuh black card who see thuh black card? You
pick thuh red card you pick a loser you pick that red card
you pick a loser you pick thuh black card thuh deuce of
spades you pick a winner who sees thuh deuce of spades
thuh one who sees it never fades watch me now as I throw

thuh cards. Red losers black winner follow thuh deuce of spades chase thuh black deuce. Dark deuce will get you thuh win.)))

> Even though Lincoln speaks softly, Booth wakes and, unbeknownst to Lincoln, listens intently.

(Rest)

Lincoln
((10 will get you 20, 20 will get you 40.))
(Rest)
((Ima show you thuh cards: 2 red cards but only one spade. Dark winner in thuh center and thuh red losers on thuh sides. Pick uh red card you got a loser pick thuh other red card you got a loser pick thuh black card you got a winner. One good pickll get you in, 2 good picks and you gone win. Watch me come on watch me now.))
(Rest)
((Who sees thuh winner who knows where its at? You do? You sure? Go on then, put yr money where yr mouth is. Put yr money down you aint no clown. No? Ah, you had thuh card but you didnt have thuh heart.))
(Rest)
((Watch me now as I throw thuh cards watch me real close. Ok, man, you know which card is the deuce of spades? Was you watching Links lighting fast express? Was you watching Link cause he the best? So you sure, huh? Point it out first, then place yr bet and Linkll show you yr winner.))
(Rest)
((500 dollars? You thuh man of thuh hour you thuh man with thuh power. You musta been watching Link real close. You must be thuh man who know thuh most. Ok. Lay the cash in my hand cause Link the man. Thank you, mister. This card you say?))
(Rest)
((Wrong! Ha!))
(Rest)
((Thats thuh show. We gotta go.))

Lincoln puts the cards down.
He moves away from the monte setup.
He sits on the edge of his easy chair,
but he can't take his eyes off the cards.

Intermission

Scene Five

Several days have passed.
Its now Wednesday night.
Booth is sitting in his brand-new suit.
The monte setup is nowhere in sight.
In its place is a table with two nice chairs.
The table is covered with a lovely tablecloth
and there are nice plates, silverware,
champagne glasses and candles.
All the makings of a very romantic dinner for two.
The whole apartment in fact takes its cue from the table.
Its been cleaned up considerably.
New curtains on the windows,
a doily-like object on the recliner.
Booth sits at the table darting his eyes around,
making sure everything is looking good.

Booth
Shit.

He notices some of his girlie magazines visible from
underneath his bed. He goes over and
nudges them out of sight. He sits back down.
He notices that theyre still visible. He goes over and nudges
them some more, kicking at them finally. Then he takes the
spread from his bed and pulls it down, hiding them.
He sits back down. He gets up.
Checks the champagne on much melted ice.
Checks the food.

Booth

Foods getting cold, Grace!! Dont worry man, she'll get here, she'll get here.

> He sits back down.
> He goes over to the bed. Checks it for springiness.
> Smoothes down the bedspread. Double-checks 2 matching
> silk dressing gowns, very expensive, marked "His" and "Hers."
> Lays the dressing gowns across the bed again.
> He sits back down. He cant help but notice the visibility of
> the girlie magazines again. He goes to the bed,
> kicks them fiercely, then on his hands and
> knees shoves them. Then he begins to get under the bed
> to push them, but he remembers his nice clothing
> and takes off his jacket. After a beat
> he removes his pants and, in this half-dressed way,
> he crawls under the bed to give those telltale
> magazines a good and final shove.
> Lincoln comes in.
> At first Booth, still stripped down to his underwear,
> thinks its his date. When he realizes its his brother,
> he does his best to keep Lincoln from entering
> the apartment. Lincoln wears his frock coat
> and carries the rest of his getup in a plastic bag.

Lincoln

You in the middle of it?

Booth

What the hell you doing here?

Lincoln

If yr in thuh middle of it I can go. Or I can just be real quiet and just—sing a song in my head or something.

Booth

The casas off limits to you tonight.

Lincoln

You know when we lived in that 2-room place with the cement backyard and the frontyard with nothing but trash in

it, Mom and Pops would do it in the middle of the night and
I would always hear them but I would sing in my head,
cause, I dunno, I couldnt bear to listen.

Booth
You gotta get out of here.

Lincoln
I would make up all kinds of songs. Oh, sorry, yr all up in it.
No sweat, bro. No sweat. Hey, Grace, howyadoing?!

Booth
She aint here yet, man. Shes running late. And its a good
thing too cause I aint all dressed yet. Yr gonna spend thuh
night with friends?

Lincoln
Yeah.

> Booth waits for Lincoln to leave. Lincoln stands his ground.

Lincoln
I lost my job.

Booth
Hunh.

Lincoln
I come in there right on time like I do every day and
that motherfucker gives me some song and dance about
cutbacks and too many folks complaining.

Booth
Hunh.

Lincoln
Showd me thuh wax dummy—hes buying it right out of
a catalog.
(Rest)
I walked out still wearing my getup.
(Rest)

I could go back in tomorrow. I could tell him I'll take another pay cut. Thatll get him to take me back.

Booth
Link. Yr free. Dont go crawling back. Yr free at last! Now you can do anything you want. Yr not tied down by that job. You can—you can do something else. Something that pays better maybe.

Lincoln
You mean Hustle.

Booth
Maybe. Hey, Graces on her way. You gotta go.

> Lincoln flops into his chair.
> Booth is waiting for him to move. Lincoln doesnt budge.

Lincoln
I'll stay until she gets here. I'll act nice. I wont embarrass you.

Booth
You gotta go.

Lincoln
What time she coming?

Booth
Shes late. She could be here any second.

Lincoln
I'll meet her. I met her years ago. I'll meet her again.
(Rest)
How late is she?

Booth
She was supposed to be here at 8.

Lincoln
Its after 2 a.m. Shes—shes late.
(Rest)

Maybe when she comes you could put the blanket over me
and I'll just pretend like Im not here.
(Rest)
I'll wait. And when she comes I'll go. I need to sit down.
I been walking around all day.

Booth
Lincoln

> Booth goes to his bed and dresses hurriedly.

Booth
Pretty nice, right? The china thuh silver thuh crystal.

Lincoln
Its great.
(Rest)
Boosted?

Booth
Yeah.

Lincoln
Thought you went and spent yr inheritance for a minute,
you had me going I was thinking shit, Booth—3-Card—that
3-Cards gone and spent his inheritance and the gal is—late.

Booth
Its boosted. Every bit of it.
(Rest)
Fuck this waiting bullshit.

Lincoln
She'll be here in a minute. Dont sweat it.

Booth
Right.

> Booth comes to the table. Sits. Relaxes as best he can.

Booth

How come I got a hand for boosting and I dont got a hand for throwing cards? Its sorta the same thing—you gotta be quick—and slick. Maybe yll show me yr moves sometime.

Lincoln
Booth
Lincoln
Booth

Lincoln

Look out the window. When you see Grace coming, I'll go.

Booth

Cool. Cause youd jinx it, youd really jinx it. Maybe you being here has jinxed it already. Naw. Shes just a little late. You aint jinxed nothing.

> Booth sits by the window,
> glancing out, watching for his date.
> Lincoln sits in his recliner. He finds the whiskey bottle,
> sips from it. He then rummages around,
> finding the raggedy photo album.
> He looks through it.

Lincoln

There we are at that house. Remember when we moved in?

Booth

No.

Lincoln

You were 2 or 3.

Booth

I was 4.

Lincoln

I was 9. We all thought it was the best fucking house in the world.

Booth

Cement backyard and a frontyard full of trash, yeah, dont be
going down memory lane man, yll jinx thuh vibe I got going
in here. Gracell be walking in here and wrinkling up her
nose cause you done jinxed up thuh joint with yr raggedy
recollections.

Lincoln

We had some great times in that house, bro. Selling lemon-
ade on thuh corner, thuh treehouse out back, summers
spent lying in thuh grass and looking at thuh stars.

Booth

We never did none of that shit.

Lincoln

But we had us some good times. That row of nails I got
you to line up behind Dads car so when he backed out the
driveway to work—

Booth

He came back that night, only time I ever seen his face go
red, 4 flat tires and yelling bout how thuh white man done
sabotaged him again.

Lincoln

And neither of us flinched. Neither of us let on that itd been us.

Booth

It was at dinner, right? What were we eating?

Lincoln

Food.

Booth

We was eating pork chops, mashed potatoes and peas.
I remember cause I had to look at them peas real hard to
keep from letting on. And I would glance over at you, not
really glancing not actually turning my head, but I was
looking at you out thuh corner of my eye. I was sure he was
gonna find us out and then he woulda whipped us good. But

I kept glancing at you and you was cool, man. Like nothing
was going on. You was cooooool.
(Rest)
What time is it?

Lincoln
After 3.
(Rest)
You should call her. Something mighta happened.

Booth
No man, Im cool. She'll be here in a minute. Patience is a
virtue. She'll be here.

Lincoln
You look sad.

Booth
Nope. Im just, you know, Im just—

Lincoln
Cool.

Booth
Yeah. Cool.

> Booth comes over, takes the bottle of whiskey and
> pours himself a big glassful. He returns to the
> window looking out and drinking.

Booth
They give you a severance package, at thuh job?

Lincoln
A weeks pay.

Booth
Great.

Lincoln
I blew it. Spent it all.

Booth

On what?

Lincoln

—. Just spent it.

(Rest)

It felt good, spending it. Felt really good. Like back in thuh
day when I was really making money. Throwing thuh cards
all day and strutting and rutting all night. Didnt have to
take no shit from no fool, didnt have to worry about getting
fired in favor of some damn wax dummy. I was thuh shit
and they was my fools.

(Rest)

Back in thuh day.

(Rest)

(Rest)

Why you think they left us, man?

Booth

Mom and Pops? I dont think about it too much.

Lincoln

I dont think they liked us.

Booth

Naw. That aint it.

Lincoln

I think there was something out there that they liked more
than they liked us and for years they was struggling against
moving towards that more liked something. Each of them
had a special something that they was struggling against.
Moms had hers. Pops had his. And they was struggling.
We moved out of that nasty apartment into a house. A whole
house. It wernt perfect but it was a house and theyd bought
it and they brought us there and everything we owned,
figuring we could be a family in that house and them things,
them two separate things each of them was struggling
against, would just leave them be. Them things would see
thuh house and be impressed and just leave them be.
Would see thuh job Pops had and how he shined his shoes

every night before he went to bed, shining them shoes whether they needed it or not, and thuh thing he was struggling against would see all that and just let him be, and thuh thing Moms was struggling against, it would see the food on the table every night and listen to her voice when she'd read to us sometimes, the clean clothes, the buttons sewed on all right and it would just let her be. Just let us all be, just regular people living in a house. That wernt too much to ask.

Booth
Least we was grown when they split.

Lincoln
16 and 11 aint grown.

Booth
16s grown. Almost. And I was ok cause you were there.
(Rest)
Shit man, it aint like they both one day both, together packed all they shit up and left us so they could have fun in thuh sun on some tropical island and you and me would have to grub in thuh dirt forever. They didnt leave together. That makes it different. She left. 2 years go by. Then he left. Like neither of them couldnt handle it no more. She split then he split. Like thuh whole family mortgage bills going to work thing was just too much. And I dont blame them. You dont see me holding down a steady job. Cause its bullshit and I know it. I seen how it cracked them up and I aint going there.
(Rest)
It aint right me trying to make myself into a one woman man just because she wants me like that. One woman rubber-wearing motherfucker. Shit. Not me. She gonna walk in here looking all hot and shit trying to see how much she can get me to sweat, how much she can get me to give her before she gives me mines. Shit.

Lincoln
Booth

Lincoln

Moms told me I shouldnt never get married.

Booth

She told me thuh same thing.

Lincoln

They gave us each 500 bucks then they cut out.

Booth

Thats what Im gonna do. Give my kids 500 bucks then cut out. Thats thuh way to do it.

Lincoln

You dont got no kids.

Booth

Im gonna have kids then Im gonna cut out.

Lincoln

Leaving each of yr offspring 500 bucks as yr splitting.

Booth

Yeah.
(Rest)
Just goes to show Mom and Pops had some agreement between them.

Lincoln

How so.

Booth

Theyd stopped talking to eachother. Theyd stopped *screwing* eachother. But they had an agreement. Somewhere in there when it looked like all they had was hate they sat down and did thuh "split" budget.
(Rest)
When Moms splits she gives me 5 hundred-dollar bills rolled up and tied up tight in one of her nylon stockings. She tells me to put it in a safe place, to spend it only in case of an emergency, and not to tell nobody I got it, not even you. 2 years later Pops splits and before he goes—

Lincoln

He slips me 10 fifties in a clean handkerchief: "Hide this somewheres good, dont go blowing it, dont tell no one you got it, especially that Booth."

Booth

Theyd been scheming together all along. They left separately but they was in agreement. Maybe they arrived at the same place at the same time, maybe they renewed they wedding vows, maybe they got another family.

Lincoln

Maybe they got 2 new kids. 2 boys. Different than us, though. Better.

Booth

Maybe.

> Their glasses are empty. The whiskey bottle is empty too.
> Booth takes the champagne bottle from the ice tub.
> He pops the cork and pours drinks for
> his brother and himself.

Booth

I didnt mind them leaving cause you was there. Thats why Im hooked on us working together. If we could work together it would be like old times. They split and we got that room downtown. You was done with school and I stopped going. And we had to run around doing odd jobs just to keep the lights on and the heat going and thuh child protection bitch off our backs. It was you and me against thuh world, Link. It could be like that again.

Lincoln
Booth
Lincoln
Booth

Lincoln

Throwing thuh cards aint as easy as it looks.

Booth

I aint stupid.

Lincoln

When you hung with us back then, you was just on thuh sidelines. Thuh perspective from thuh sidelines is thuh perspective of a customer. There was all kinds of things you didnt know nothing about.

Booth

Lonny would entice folks into thuh game as they walked by. Thuh 2 folks on either side of ya looked like they was playing but they was only pretending tuh play. Just tuh generate excitement. You was moving thuh cards as fast as you could hoping that yr hands would be faster than yr customers eyes. Sometimes you won sometimes you lost what else is there to know?

Lincoln

Thuh customer is actually called the "Mark." You know why?

Booth

Cause hes thuh one you got yr eye on. You mark him with yr eye.

Lincoln
Lincoln

Booth

Im right, right?

Lincoln

Lemmie show you a few moves. If you pick up these yll have a chance.

Booth

Yr playing.

Lincoln

Get thuh cards and set it up.

Booth

No shit.

Lincoln

Set it up set it up.

>   In a flash, Booth clears away the romantic table setting
>   by gathering it all up in the tablecloth and tossing it aside.
>   As he does so he reveals the "table" underneath:
>   the 2 stacked monte milk crates
>   and the cardboard playing surface.
>   Lincoln lays out the cards. The brothers are ready.
>   Lincoln begins to teach Booth in earnest.

Lincoln

Thuh deuce of spades is thuh card tuh watch.

Booth

I work with thuh deuce of hearts. But spades is cool.

Lincoln

Theres thuh Dealer, thuh Stickman, thuh Sides, thuh
Lookout and thuh Mark. I'll be thuh Dealer.

Booth

I'll be thuh Lookout. Lemmie be thuh Lookout, right? I'll
keep an eye for thuh cops. I got my piece in my pants.

Lincoln

You got it on you right now?

Booth

I always carry it.

Lincoln

Even on a date? In yr own home?

Booth

You never know, man.
(Rest)
So Im thuh Lookout.

Lincoln
Gimmie yr piece.

> Booth gives Lincoln his gun. Lincoln moves
> the little wooden chair to face right in front of the setup.
> He then puts the gun on the chair.

Lincoln
We dont need nobody standing on the corner watching for cops cause there aint none. Thatll be the lookout.

Booth
I'll be thuh Stickman, then.

Lincoln
Stickman knows the game inside out. You aint there yet. But you will be. You wanna learn good, be my Sideman. Playing along with the Dealer, moving the Mark to lay his money down. You wanna learn, right?

Booth
I'll be thuh Side.

Lincoln
Good.
(Rest)
First thing you learn is what is. Next thing you learn is what aint. You dont know what is you dont know what aint, you dont know shit.

Booth
Right.

Lincoln
Booth

Booth
Whatchu looking at?

Lincoln
Im sizing you up.

Booth
Oh yeah?!

Lincoln
Dealer always sizes up thuh crowd.

Booth
Im yr Side, Link, Im on yr team, you dont go sizing up yr own team. You save looks like that for yr Mark.

Lincoln
Dealer always sizes up thuh crowd. Everybody out there is part of the crowd. His crew is part of the crowd, he himself is part of the crowd. Dealer always sizes up thuh crowd.

> Lincoln looks Booth over some more then looks around at an imaginary crowd.

Booth
Then what then what?

Lincoln
Dealer dont wanna play.

Booth
Bullshit man! Come on you promised!

Lincoln
Thats thuh Dealers attitude. He *acts* like he dont wanna play. He holds back and thuh crowd, with their eagerness to see his skill and their willingness to take a chance, and their greediness to win his cash, the larceny in their hearts, all goad him on and push him to throw his cards, although of course the Dealer has been wanting to throw his cards all along. Only he dont never show it.

Booth
Thats some sneaky shit, Link.

Lincoln
It sets thuh mood. You wanna have them in yr hand before you deal a hand, K?

Booth
Cool. —K.

Lincoln
Right.

Lincoln
Booth

Booth
You sizing me up again?

Lincoln
Theres 2 parts to throwing thuh cards. Both parts are fairly complicated. Thuh moves and thuh grooves, thuh talk and thuh walk, thuh patter and thuh pitter pat, thuh flap and thuh rap: what yr doing with yr mouth and what yr doing with yr hands.

Booth
I got thuh words down pretty good.

Lincoln
You need to work on both.

Booth
K.

Lincoln
A goodlooking walk and a dynamite talk captivates their entire attention. The Mark focuses with 2 organs primarily: his eyes and his ears. Leave one out you lose yr shirt. Captivate both, yr golden.

Booth
So them times I seen you lose, them times I seen thuh Mark best you, that was a time when yr hands werent fast enough or yr patter werent right.

Lincoln
You could say that.

Booth
So, there was plenty of times—

Lincoln moves the cards around.

Lincoln
You see what Im doing? Dont look at my hands, man, look at my eyes. Know what is and know what aint.

Booth
What is?

Lincoln
My eyes.

Booth
What aint?

Lincoln
My hands. Look at my eyes not my hands. And you standing there thinking how thuh fuck I gonna learn how tuh throw thuh cards if I be looking in his eyes? Look into my eyes and get yr focus. Dont think about learning how tuh throw thuh cards. Dont think about nothing. Just look into my eyes. Get yr focus.

Booth
Theyre red.

Lincoln
Look into my eyes.

Booth
You been crying?

Lincoln
Just look into my eyes, fool. Now. Look down at thuh cards. I been moving and moving and moving them around. Ready?

Booth
Yeah.

Lincoln
Ok, Sideman, thuh Marks got his eye on you. Yr gonna show him its easy.

Booth
K.

Lincoln
Pick out thuh deuce of spades. Dont pick it up just point to it.

Booth
This one, right?

Lincoln
Dont ask thuh Dealer if yr right, man, point to yr card with confidence.

> Booth points.

Booth
That one.
(Rest)
Flip it over, man.

> Lincoln flips over the card. It is in fact
> the deuce of spades. Booth struts around gloating
> like a rooster. Lincoln is mildly crestfallen.

Booth
Am I right or am I right?! Make room for 3-Card! Here comes thuh champ!

Lincoln
Cool. Stay focused. Now we gonna add the second element. Listen.

> Lincoln moves the cards and
> speaks in a low hypnotic voice.

Lincoln

Lean in close and watch me now: who see thuh black card who see thuh black card I see thuh black card black cards thuh winner pick thuh black card thats thuh winner pick thuh red card thats thuh loser pick thuh other red card thats thuh other loser pick thuh black card you pick thuh winner. Watch me as I throw thuh cards. Here we go.

(Rest)

Who see thuh black card who see thuh black card? You pick thuh red card you pick a loser you pick that red card you pick a loser you pick thuh black card thuh deuce of spades you pick a winner who sees thuh deuce of spades thuh one who sees it never fades watch me now as I throw thuh cards. Red losers black winner follow thuh deuce of spades chase thuh black deuce. Dark deuce will get you thuh win. One good pickll get you in 2 good picks you gone win. 10 will get you 20, 20 will get you 40.

(Rest)

Ima show you thuh cards: 2 red cards but only one spade. Dark winner in thuh center and thuh red losers on thuh sides. Pick uh red card you got a loser pick thuh other red card you got a loser pick thuh black card you got a winner. Watch me watch me watch me now.

(Rest)

Ok, 3-Card, you know which cards thuh deuce of spades?

Booth

Yeah.

Lincoln

You sure? Yeah? You sure you sure or you just think you sure? Oh you sure you sure huh? Was you watching Links lighting fast express? Was you watching Link cause he the best? So you sure, huh? Point it out. Now, place yr bet and Linkll turn over yr card.

Booth

What should I bet?

Lincoln

Dont bet nothing man, we just playing. Slap me 5 and point out thuh deuce.

Booth

Yeah, baby! 3-Card got thuh moves! You didnt know lil bro
had thuh stuff, huh? Think again, Link, think again.

Lincoln

You wanna learn or you wanna run yr mouth?

Booth

Thought you had fast hands. Wassup? What happened tuh
"Links Lightning Fast Express"? Turned into uh local train
looks like tuh me.

Lincoln

Thats yr whole motherfucking problem. Yr so busy running
yr mouth you aint never gonna learn nothing! You think you
something but you aint shit.

Booth

I aint shit, I am _The_ Shit. Shit. Wheres thuh dark deuce?
Right there! Yes, baby!

Lincoln

Ok, 3-Card. Cool. Lets switch. Take thuh cards and show
me whatcha got. Go on. Dont touch thuh cards too heavy
just—its a light touch. Like yr touching Graces skin.
Or, whatever, man, just a light touch. Like uh whisper.

Booth

Like uh whisper.

Booth moves the cards around,
in an awkward imitation of his brother.

Lincoln

Good.

Booth

Yeah. All right. Look into my eyes.

Booths speech is loud and his movements are jerky.
He is doing worse than when he threw
the cards at the top of the play.

Booth

Watch-me-close-watch-me-close-now: who-see-thuh-black-card-who-see-thuh-black-card? I-see-thuh-black-card. Here-it-is. Thuh-black-card-is-thuh-winner. Pick-thuh-black-card-and-you-pick-uh-winner. Pick-uh-red-card-and-you-pick-uh-loser. Theres-thuh-loser-yeah-theres-thuh-red-card, theres-thuh-other-loser-and-theres-thuh-black-card, thuh-winner. Watch-me-close-watch-me-close-now: 3-Card-throws-thuh-cards-lightning-fast. 3-Card-thats-me-and-Ima-last. Watch-me-throw-cause-here-I-go. See thuh black card? Yeah? Who see I see you see thuh black card?

Lincoln

Hahahahhahahahahahahah!

Lincoln doubles over laughing.
Booth puts on his coat and pockets his gun.

Booth

What?

Lincoln

Nothing, man, nothing.

Booth

What?!

Lincoln

Yr just, yr just a little wild with it. You talk like that on thuh street cards or no cards and theyll lock you up, man. Shit. Reminds me of that time when you hung with us and we let you try being thuh Stick cause you wanted to so bad. Thuh hustle was so simple. Remember? I told you that when I put my hand in my left pocket you was to get thuh Mark tuh pick thuh card on that side. You got to thinking something like Links left means my left some dyslexic shit and turned thuh wrong card. There was 800 bucks on the line and you fucked it up.

(Rest)
But it was cool, little bro, cause we made the money back.
It worked out cool.
(Rest)
So, yeah, I said a light touch, little bro. Throw thuh cards
light. Like uh whisper.

Booth
Like Graces skin.

Lincoln
Like Graces skin.

Booth
What time is it?

> Lincoln holds up his watch. Booth takes a look.

Booth
Bitch. *Bitch!* She said she was gonna show up around 8.
8-a-fucking-clock.

Lincoln
Maybe she meant 8 *a.m.*

Booth
Yeah. She gonna come all up in my place talking bout how
she *love* me. How she cant stop *thinking* bout me. Nother
mans shit up in her nother mans thing in her nother mans
dick on her breath.

Lincoln
Maybe something happened to her.

Booth
Something happened to her all right. She trying to make a
chump outa me. I aint her chump. I aint nobodys chump.

Lincoln
Sit. I'll go to the payphone on the corner. I'll—

Booth

Thuh world puts its foot in yr face and you dont move. You tell thuh world tuh keep on stepping. But Im my own man, Link. I aint you.

> Booth goes out, slamming the door behind him.

Lincoln

You got that right.

> After a moment Lincoln picks up the cards.
> He moves them around fast, faster, faster.

Scene Six

Thursday night.
The room looks empty, as if neither brother is home.
Lincoln comes in.
Hes high on liquor. He strides in,
leaving the door slightly ajar.

Lincoln
Taaadaaaa!
(Rest)
(Rest)
Taadaa, motherfucker. Taadaa!
(Rest)
Booth—uh, 3-Card—you here? Nope. Good. Just as well.
Ha Ha *Ha Ha Ha*!

He pulls an enormous wad of money
from his pocket. He counts it, slowly and luxuriously,
arranging and smoothing the bills
and sounding the amounts under his breath.
He neatly rolls up the money, secures it with a rubber band
and puts it back in his pocket. He relaxes in his chair.
Then he takes the money out again, counting it
all over again, but this time quickly,
with the touch of an expert hustler.

Lincoln
You didnt go back, Link, you got back, you got it back you
got yr shit back in thuh saddle, man, you got back in
business. Walking in Luckys and you seen how they was

looking at you? Lucky starts pouring for you when you walk in. And the women. You see how they was looking at you? Bought drinks for everybody. Bought drinks for Lucky. Bought drinks for Luckys damn dog. Shit. And thuh women be hanging on me and purring. And I be feeling that old call of thuh wild calling. I got more phone numbers in my pockets between thuh time I walked out that door and thuh time I walked back in than I got in my whole life. Cause my shit is *back*. And back better than it was when it left too. Shoot. Who thuh man? Link. Thats right. Purrrrring all up on me and letting me touch them and promise them shit. 3 of them sweethearts in thuh restroom on my dick all at once and I was *there* my shit was there. And Cookie just went out of my mind which is cool which is very cool. 3 of them. Fighting over it. Shit. Cause they knew I'd been throwing thuh cards. Theyd seen me on thuh corner with thuh old crew or if they aint seed me with they own eyes theyd heard word. Links thuh stink! Theyd heard word and they seed uh sad face on some poor sucker or a tear in thuh eye of some stupid fucking tourist and they figured it was me whod just took thuh suckers last dime, it was me who had all thuh suckers loot. They knew. They knew.

> Booth appears in the room. He was standing
> behind the screen, unseen all this time.
> He goes to the door, soundlessly, just stands there.

Lincoln
And they was all in Luckys. Shit. And they was waiting for me to come in from my last throw. Cant take too many fools in one day, its bad luck, Link, so they was all waiting in there for me to come in thuh door and let thuh liquor start flowing and thuh music start going and let thuh boys who dont have thuh balls to get nothing but a regular job and uh weekly paycheck, let them crowd around and get in some-how on thuh excitement, and make way for thuh ladies, so they can run they hands on my clothes and feel thuh magic and imagine thuh man, with plenty to go around, living and breathing underneath.
(Rest)

They all thought I was down and out! They all thought I was some NoCount HasBeen LostCause motherfucker. But I got my shit back. Thats right. They stepped on me and kept right on stepping. Not no more. Who thuh man?! Goddamnit, who thuh—

Booth closes the door.

Lincoln
Booth

(Rest)

Lincoln
Another evening to remember, huh?

Booth
(Rest)
Uh—yeah, man, yeah. Thats right, thats right.

Lincoln
Had me a memorable evening myself.

Booth
I got news.
(Rest)
What you been up to?

Lincoln
Yr news first.

Booth
Its good.

Lincoln
Yeah?

Booth
Yeah.

Lincoln
Go head then.

Booth
(Rest)
Grace got down on her knees. Down on her knees, man.
Asked *me* tuh marry *her*.

Lincoln
Shit.

Booth
Amazing Grace!

Lincoln
Lucky you, man.

Booth
And guess where she was, I mean, while I was here waiting
for her. She was over at her house watching tv. I'd told her
come over Thursday and I got it all wrong and was thinking
I said Wednesday and here I was sitting waiting my ass off
and all she was doing was over at her house just watching tv.

Lincoln
Howboutthat.

Booth
She wants to get married right away. Shes tired of waiting.
Feels her clock ticking and shit. Wants to have my baby.
But dont look so glum man, we gonna have a boy and we
gonna name it after you.

Lincoln
Thats great, man. Thats really great.

Booth
Lincoln

Booth
Whats yr news?

Lincoln
(Rest)
Nothing.

Booth
Mines good news, huh?

Lincoln
Yeah. Real good news, bro.

Booth
Bad news is—well, shes real set on us living together. And she always did like this place.
(Rest)
Yr gonna have to leave. Sorry.

Lincoln
No sweat.

Booth
This was only a temporary situation anyhow.

Lincoln
No sweat man. You got a new life opening up for you, no sweat. Graces moving in today? I can leave right now.

Booth
I dont mean to put you out.

Lincoln
No sweat. I'll just pack up.

> Lincoln rummages around finding a suitcase
> and begins to pack his things.

Booth
Just like that, huh? "No sweat"?! Yesterday you lost yr damn job. You dont got no cash. You dont got no friends, no nothing, but you clearing out just like that and its "no sweat"?!

Lincoln
Youve been real generous and you and Grace need me gone and its time I found my own place.

Booth

No sweat.

Lincoln

No sweat.
(Rest)
K. I'll spill it. I got another job, so getting my own place aint gonna be so bad.

Booth

You got a new job! Doing what?

Lincoln

Security guard.

Booth

(Rest)
Security guard. Howaboutthat.

> Lincoln continues packing the few things he has.
> He picks up a whiskey bottle.

Booth

Go head, take thuh med-sin, bro. You gonna need it more than me. I got, you know, I got my love to keep me warm and shit.

Lincoln

You gonna have to get some kind of work, or are you gonna let Grace support you?

Booth

I got plans.

Lincoln

She might want you now but she wont want you for long if you dont get some kind of job. Shes a smart chick. And she cares about you. But she aint gonna let you treat her like some pack mule while shes out working her ass off and yr laying up in here scheming and dreaming to cover up thuh fact that you dont got no skills.

Booth
Grace is very cool with who I am and where Im at, thank you.

Lincoln
It was just some advice. But, hey, yr doing great just like yr doing.

Lincoln
Booth
Lincoln
Booth

Booth
When Pops left he didnt take nothing with him. I always thought that was fucked-up.

Lincoln
He was a drunk. Everything he did was always half regular and half fucked-up.

Booth
Whyd he leave his clothes though? Even drunks gotta wear clothes.

Lincoln
Whyd he leave his clothes whyd he leave us? He was uh drunk, bro. He—whatever, right? I mean, you aint gonna figure it out by thinking about it. Just call it one of thuh great unsolved mysteries of existence.

Booth
Moms had a man on thuh side.

Lincoln
Yeah? Pops had side shit going on too. More than one.
He would take me with him when he went to visit them. Yeah.
(Rest)
Sometimes he'd let me meet the ladies. They was all very nice. Very polite. Most of them real pretty. Sometimes he'd let me watch. Most of thuh time I was just outside on thuh porch or in thuh lobby or in thuh car waiting for him but sometimes he'd let me watch.

Booth
What was it like?

Lincoln
Nothing. It wasnt like nothing. He made it seem like it was
this big deal this great thing he was letting me witness but it
wasnt like nothing.
(Rest)
One of his ladies liked me, so I would do her after he'd done
her. On thuh sly though. He'd be laying there, spent and
sleeping and snoring and her and me would be sneaking it.

Booth
Shit.

Lincoln
It was alright.

Booth
Lincoln

> Lincoln takes his crumpled Abe Lincoln getup
> from the closet. Isnt sure what to do with it.

Booth
Im gonna miss you—coming home in that getup. I dont
even got a picture of you in it for the album.

Lincoln
(Rest)
Hell, I'll put it on. Get thuh camera get thuh camera.

Booth
Yeah?

Lincoln
What thuh fuck, right?

Booth
Yeah, what thuh fuck.

> Booth scrambles around the apartment
> and finds the camera.
> Lincoln quickly puts on the getup,
> including 2 thin smears of white pancake makeup,
> more like war paint than whiteface.

Lincoln
They didnt fire me cause I wasnt no good. They fired me cause they was cutting back. Me getting dismissed didnt have no reflection on my performance. And I was a damn good Honest Abe considering.

Booth
Yeah. You look great man, really great. Fix yr hat. Get in thuh light. Smile.

Lincoln
Lincoln didnt never smile.

Booth
Sure he smiled.

Lincoln
No he didnt, man, you seen thuh pictures of him. In all his pictures he was real serious.

Booth
You got a new job, yr having a good day, right?

Lincoln
Yeah.

Booth
So smile.

Lincoln
Snapshots gonna look pretty stupid with me—

> Booth takes a picture.

Booth
Thisll look great in thuh album.

Lincoln
Lets take one together, you and me.

Booth
No thanks. Save the film for the wedding.

Lincoln
This wasnt a bad job. I just outgrew it. I could put in a word
for you down there, maybe when business picks up again
theyd hire you.

Booth
No thanks. That shit aint for me. I aint into pretending Im
someone else all day.

Lincoln
I was just sitting there in thuh getup. I wasnt pretending
nothing.

Booth
What was going on in yr head?

Lincoln
I would make up songs and shit.

Booth
And think about women.

Lincoln
Sometimes.

Booth
Cookie.

Lincoln
Sometimes.

Booth
And how she came over here one night looking for you.

Lincoln
I was at Luckys.

Booth
She didnt know that.

Lincoln
I was drinking.

Booth
All she knew was you couldnt get it up. You couldnt get it up with her so in her head you was tired of her and had gone out to screw somebody new and this time maybe werent never coming back.
(Rest)
She had me pour her a drink or 2. I didnt want to. She wanted to get back at you by having some fun of her own and when I told her to go out and have it, she said she wanted to have her fun right here. With me.
(Rest)
And then, just like that, she changed her mind.
(Rest)
But she'd hooked me. That bad part of me that I fight down everyday. You beat yrs down and it stays there dead but mine keeps coming up for another round. And the bad part of me took her clothing off and carried her into thuh bed and had her, Link, yr Cookie. It wasnt just thuh bad part of me it was all of me, man, I had her. Yr damn wife. Right in that bed.

Lincoln
I used to think about her all thuh time but I dont think about her no more.

Booth
I told her if she dumped you I'd marry her but I changed my mind.

Lincoln
I dont think about her no more.

Booth
You dont go back.

Lincoln
Nope.

Booth

Cause you cant. No matter what you do you cant get back to being who you was. Best you can do is just pretend to be yr old self.

Lincoln

Yr outa yr mind.

Booth

Least Im still me!

Lincoln

Least I work. You never did like to work. You better come up with some kinda way to bring home the bacon or Gracell drop you like a hot rock.

Booth

I got plans!

Lincoln

Yeah, you gonna throw thuh cards, right?

Booth

Thats right!

Lincoln

You a double left-handed motherfucker who dont stand a chance in all get out out there throwing no cards.

Booth

You scared. You scared I got yr shit.

Lincoln

You aint never gonna do nothing.

Booth

You scared you gonna throw and Ima kick yr ass—like yr boss kicked yr ass like yr wife kicked yr ass—then Ima go out there and do thuh cards like you do and Ima be thuh man and you aint gonna be shit.

(Rest)
Ima set it up. And you gonna throw. Or are you scared?

Lincoln
Im gone.

Lincoln goes to leave.

Booth
Fuck that!

Lincoln
Booth

Lincoln
Damn. I didnt know it went so deep for you lil bro. Set up
the cards.

Booth
Thought you was gone.

Lincoln
Set it up.

Booth
Ima kick yr ass.

Lincoln
Set it up!

Booth hurriedly sets up the milk crates and cardboard top.
Lincoln throws the cards.

Lincoln
Lean in close and watch me now: who see thuh black card
who see thuh black card I see thuh black card black cards
thuh winner pick thuh black card thats thuh winner pick
thuh red card thats thuh loser pick thuh other red card thats
thuh other loser pick thuh black card you pick thuh winner.
Who see thuh black card who see thuh black card? You
pick thuh red card you pick a loser you pick that red card

you pick a loser you pick thuh black card thuh deuce of spades you pick a winner who sees thuh deuce of spades thuh one who sees it never fades watch me now as I throw thuh cards. Red losers black winner follow thuh deuce of spades chase thuh black deuce. Dark deuce will get you thuh win. 10 will get you 20, 20 will get you 40. One good pickll get you in 2 good picks and you gone win.
(Rest)
Ok, man, wheres thuh black deuce?

> Booth points to a card. Lincoln flips it over.
> It is the deuce of spades.

Booth
Who thuh man?!

> Lincoln turns over the other 2 cards,
> looking at them confusedly.

Lincoln
Hhhhh.

Booth
Who thuh man, Link?! Huh? Who thuh man, Link?!?!

Lincoln
You thuh man, man.

Booth
I got yr shit down.

Lincoln
Right.

Booth
"Right"? All you saying is "right"?
(Rest)
You was out on the street throwing. Just today. Werent you? You wasnt gonna tell me.

Lincoln
Tell you what?

Booth

That you was out throwing.

Lincoln

I was gonna tell you, sure. Cant go and leave my little bro
out thuh loop, can I? Didnt say nothing cause I thought you
heard. Did all right today but Im still rusty, I guess.
But hey—yr getting good.

Booth

But I'll get out there on thuh street and still fuck up, wont I?

Lincoln

You seem pretty good, bro.

Booth

You gotta do it for real, man.

Lincoln

I am doing it for real. And yr getting good.

Booth

I dunno. It didnt feel real. Kinda felt—well it didnt feel real.

Lincoln

We're missing the essential elements. The crowd, the street,
thuh traffic sounds, all that.

Booth

We missing something else too, thuh thing thatll really
make it real.

Lincoln

Whassat, bro?

Booth

Thuh cash. Its just bullshit without thuh money. Put some
money down on thuh table then itd be real, then youd do it
for real, then I'd win it for real.
(Rest)
And dont be looking all glum like that. I know you got money.
A whole pocketful. Put it down.

Lincoln
Booth

Booth
You scared of losing it to thuh man, chump? Put it down,
less you think thuh kid who got two left hands is gonna give
you uh left hook. Put it down, bro, put it down.

> Lincoln takes the roll of bills from his pocket
> and places it on the table.

Booth
How much you got there?

Lincoln
500 bucks.

Booth
Cool.
(Rest)
Ready?

Lincoln
Does it feel real?

Booth
Yeah. Clean slate. Take it from the top. "One good pickll get
you in 2 good picks and you gone win."
(Rest)
Go head.

Lincoln
Watch me now:

Booth
Woah, man, woah.
(Rest)
You think Ima chump.

Lincoln
No I dont.

Booth
You aint going full out.

Lincoln
I was just getting started.

Booth
But when you got good and started you wasnt gonna go full
out. You wasnt gonna go all out. You was gonna do thuh
pussy shit, not thuh real shit.

Lincoln
I put my money down. Money makes it real.

Booth
But not if I dont put no money down tuh match it.

Lincoln
You dont got no money.

Booth
I got money!

Lincoln
You aint worked in years. You dont got shit.

Booth
I got money.

Lincoln
Whatcha been doing, skimming off my weekly paycheck
and squirreling it away?

Booth
I got money.
(Rest)

> They stand there sizing eachother up. Booth breaks away,
> going over to his hiding place from which he gets
> an old nylon stocking with money in the toe,
> a knot holding the money secure.

Lincoln
Booth

Booth

You know she was putting her stuff in plastic bags? She was
just putting her stuff in plastic bags not putting but shoving.
She was shoving her stuff in plastic bags and I was standing
in thuh doorway watching her and she was so busy shoving
thuh shit she didnt see me. "I aint made of money," thats
what he always saying. The guy she had on the side. I would
catch them together sometimes. Thuh first time I cut school
I got tired of hanging out so I goes home—figured I could
tell Mom I was sick and cover my ass. Come in thuh house
real slow cause Im sick and moving slow and quiet. He had
her bent over. They both had all they clothes on like they
was about to do something like go out dancing cause they
was dressed to thuh 9s but at thuh last minute his pants had
fallen down and her dress had flown up and theyd ended up
doing something else.
(Rest)
They didnt see me come in, they didnt see me watching
them, they didnt see me going out. That was uh Thursday.
Something told me tuh cut school thuh next Thursday and
sure enough—. He was her Thursday man. Every Thursday.
Yeah. And Thursday nights she was always all cleaned up
and fresh and smelling nice. Serving up dinner. And Pops
would grab her cause she was all bright and she would look
at me, like she didnt know that I knew but she was asking
me not to tell nohow. She was asking me to—oh who knows.
(Rest)
She was talking with him one day, her sideman, her
Thursday dude, her backdoor man, she needed some money
for something, thered been some kind of problem some kind
of mistake had been made some kind of mistake that needed
cleaning up and she was asking Mr. Thursday for some
money to take care of it. "I aint made of money," he says.
He was putting his foot down. And then there she was 2
months later not showing yet, maybe she'd got rid of it
maybe she hadnt maybe she'd stuffed it along with all her
other things in them plastic bags while he waited outside in
thuh car with thuh motor running. She musta known I was

gonna walk in on her this time cause she had my payoff—
my *inheritance*—she had it all ready for me. 500 dollars in
a nylon stocking. Huh.

> He places the stuffed nylon stocking
> on the table across from Lincolns money roll.

Booth
Now its real.

Lincoln
Dont put that down.

Booth
Throw thuh cards.

Lincoln
I dont want to play.

Booth
Throw thuh fucking cards, man!!

Lincoln
(Rest)
2 red cards but only one black. Pick thuh black you pick
thuh winner. All thuh cards are face down you point out
thuh cards and then you move them around. Now watch me
now, now watch me real close. Put thuh winning deuce
down in the center put thuh loser reds on either side then
you just move thuh cards around. Move them slow or move
them fast, Links thuh king he gonna last.
(Rest)
Wheres thuh deuce of spades?

> Booth chooses a card and chooses correctly.

Booth
HA!

Lincoln
One good pickll get you in 2 good picks and you gone win.

Booth
I know man I know.

Lincoln
Im just doing thuh talk.

Booth
Throw thuh fucking cards!

                                        Lincoln throws the cards.

Lincoln
Lean in close and watch me now: who see thuh black card
who see thuh black card I see thuh black card black cards
thuh winner pick thuh black card thats thuh winner pick
thuh red card thats thuh loser pick thuh other red card thats
thuh other loser pick thuh black card you pick thuh winner.
Watch me as I throw thuh cards. Here we go.
(Rest)
Ima show you thuh cards: 2 red cards but only one spade.
Dark winner in thuh center and thuh red losers on thuh
sides. Pick uh red card you got a loser pick thuh other red
card you got a loser pick thuh black card you got a winner.
Watch me watch me watch me now.
(Rest)
Who see thuh black card who see thuh black card? You
pick thuh red card you pick a loser you pick that red card
you pick a loser you pick thuh black card thuh deuce of
spades you pick a winner who sees thuh deuce of spades
thuh one who sees it never fades watch me now as I throw
thuh cards. Red losers black winner follow thuh deuce of
spades chase thuh black deuce. Dark deuce will get you
thuh win.
(Rest)
Ok, 3-Card, you know which cards thuh deuce of spades?
This is for real now, man. You pick wrong Im in yr wad and
I keep mines.

Booth
I pick right I got yr shit.

Lincoln
Yeah.

Booth
Plus I beat you for real.

Lincoln
Yeah.
(Rest)
You think we're really brothers?

Booth
Huh?

Lincoln
I know we *brothers*, but is we really brothers, you know, blood brothers or not, you and me, whatduhyathink?

Booth
I think we're brothers.

Booth
Lincoln
Booth
Lincoln
Booth
Lincoln

Lincoln
Go head man, wheres thuh deuce?

In a flash Booth points out a card.

Lincoln
You sure?

Booth
Im sure!

Lincoln
Yeah? Dont touch thuh cards, now.

Booth

Im sure.

> The 2 brothers lock eyes. Lincoln turns over the card that
> Booth selected and Booth, in a desperate break
> of concentration, glances down to see
> that he has chosen the wrong card.

Lincoln

Deuce of hearts, bro. Im sorry. Thuh deuce of spades was
this one.
(Rest)
I guess all this is mines.

> He slides the money toward himself.

Lincoln

You were almost right. Better luck next time.
(Rest)
Aint yr fault if yr eyes aint fast. And you cant help it if you
got 2 left hands, right? Throwing cards aint thuh whole
world. You got other shit going for you. You got Grace.

Booth

Right.

Lincoln

Whassamatter?

Booth

Mm.

Lincoln

Whatsup?

Booth

Nothing.

Lincoln

(Rest)
It takes a certain kind of understanding to be able to play
this game.

(Rest)
I still got thuh moves, dont I?

Booth
Yeah you still got thuh moves.

> Lincoln cant help himself. He chuckles.

Lincoln
I aint laughing at you, bro, Im just laughing. Shit there is so much to this game. This game is—there is just so much to it.

> Lincoln, still chuckling, flops down
> in the easy chair. He takes up the nylon stocking
> and fiddles with the knot.

Lincoln
Woah, she sure did tie this up tight, didnt she?

Booth
Yeah. I aint opened it since she gived it to me.

Lincoln
Yr kidding. 500 and you aint never opened it? Shit. Sure is tied tight. She said heres 500 bucks and you didnt undo thuh knot to get a look at the cash? You aint needed to take a peek in all these years? Shit. I woulda opened it right away. Just a little peek.

Booth
I been saving it.
(Rest)
Oh, dont open it, man.

Lincoln
How come?

Booth
You won it man, you dont gotta go opening it.

Lincoln
We gotta see whats in it.

Booth

We _know_ whats in it. Dont open it.

Lincoln

You are a chump, bro. There could be millions in here!
There could be nothing! I'll open it.

Booth

Dont.

Lincoln
Booth

(Rest)

Lincoln

Shit this knot aint coming out. I could cut it, but that
would spoil the whole effect, wouldnt it? Shit. Sorry. I aint
laughing at you Im just laughing. Theres so much about
those cards. You think you can learn them just by watching
and just by playing but there is more to them cards than
that. And——. Tell me something, Mr. 3-Card, she handed
you this stocking and she said there was money in it and
then she split and you say you didnt open it. Howd you
know she was for real?

Booth

She was for real.

Lincoln

How you know? She coulda been jiving you, bro. Jiving
you that there really *was* money in this thing. Jiving you
big time. Its like thuh cards. And ooooh you certainly was
persistent. But you was in such a hurry to learn thuh last
move that you didnt bother learning thuh first one. That was
yr mistake. Cause its thuh first move that separates thuh
Player from thuh Played. And thuh first move is to know
that there aint no winning. Taadaaa! It may look like you got
a chance but the only time you pick right is when thuh man
lets you. And when its thuh real deal, when its thuh real
fucking deal, bro, and thuh moneys on thuh line, thats when

thuh man wont want you picking right. He will want you picking wrong so he will make you pick wrong. Wrong wrong wrong. Ooooh, you thought you was finally happening, didnt you? You thought yr ship had come in or some shit, huh? Thought you was uh Player. But I played you, bro.

Booth
Fuck you. Fuck you FUCK YOU *FUCK YOU*!!

Lincoln
Whatever, man. Damn this knot is tough. Ima cut it.

> Lincoln reaches in his boot, pulling out a knife.
> He chuckles all the while.

Lincoln
Im not laughing at you, bro, Im just laughing.

> Booth chuckles with him.
> Lincoln holds the knife high, ready to cut the stocking.

Lincoln
Turn yr head. You may not wanna look.

> Booth turns away slightly. They both continue laughing.
> Lincoln brings the knife down to cut the stocking.

Booth
I popped her.

Lincoln
Huh?

Booth
Grace. I popped her. Grace.
(Rest)
Who thuh fuck she think she is doing me like she done? Telling me I dont got nothing going on. I showed her what I got going on. Popped her good. Twice. 3 times. Whatever.
(Rest)

She aint dead.

(Rest)

She werent wearing my ring I gived her. Said it was too small. Fuck that. Said it hurt her. Fuck that. Said she was into bigger things. *Fuck* that. Shes alive not to worry, she aint going out that easy, shes alive shes shes—.

Lincoln

Dead. Shes—

Booth

Dead.

Lincoln

Ima give you back yr stocking, man. Here, bro—

Booth

Only so long I can stand that little brother shit. Can only take it so long. Im telling you—

Lincoln

Take it back, man—

Booth

That little bro shit had to go—

Lincoln

Cool—

Booth

Like Booth went—

Lincoln

Here, 3-Card—

Booth

That Booth shit is over. 3-Cards thuh man now—

Lincoln

Ima give you yr stocking back, 3-Card—

Booth

Who thuh man now, huh? Who thuh man now?! Think you can fuck with me, motherfucker think again motherfucker think again! Think you can take me like Im just some chump some two lefthanded pussy dickbreath chump who you can take and then go laugh at. Aint laughing at me you was just laughing bunch uh bullshit and you know it.

Lincoln

Here. Take it.

Booth

I aint gonna be needing it. Go on. You won it you open it.

Lincoln

No thanks.

Booth

Open it open it open it open it. *OPEN IT!!!*
(Rest)
Open it up, bro.

Lincoln
Booth

> Lincoln brings the knife down to cut the stocking.
> In a flash, Booth grabs Lincoln from behind.
> He pulls his gun and thrusts it into
> the left side of Lincolns neck.
> They stop there poised.

Lincoln
Dont.

> Booth shoots Lincoln.
> Lincoln slumps forward, falling out of his chair and
> onto the floor. He lies there dead.
> Booth paces back and forth, like a panther
> in a cage, holding his gun.

Booth

Think you can take my shit? My shit. That shit was mines.
I kept it. Saved it. All this while. Through thick and through
thin. Through fucking thick and through fucking thin,
motherfucker. And you just gonna come up in here and
mock my shit and call me two lefthanded talking bout how
she coulda been jiving me then go steal from me? My
inheritance. You stole my *inheritance*, man. That aint right.
That aint right and you know it. You had yr own. And you
blew it. You *blew it*, motherfucker! I saved mines and you
blew yrs. Thinking you all that and blew yr shit. And
I *saved* mines.
(Rest)
You aint gonna be needing yr fucking money-roll no more,
dead motherfucker, so I will pocket it thank you.
(Rest)
Watch me close watch me close now: Ima go out there and
make a name for myself that dont have nothing to do with
you. And 3-Cards gonna be in everybodys head and in
everybodys mouth like Link was.
(Rest)
Ima take back my inheritance too. It was mines anyhow.
Even when you stole it from me it was still mines cause she
gave it to me. She didnt give it to you. And I been saving it
all this while.

> He bends to pick up the money-filled stocking.
> Then he just crumples. As he sits beside Lincolns body,
> the money-stocking falls away.
> Booth holds Lincolns body,
> hugging him close. He sobs.

Booth
AAAAAAAAAAAAAAAAAAAAH!

End of Play